The Male in A

Psychoanalytic and Cul
Perspectives

Edited by

Anastasios Gaitanidis

First published 2012 by
PALGRAVE MACMILLAN

Palgrave Macmillan in the UK is an imprint of Macmillan Publishers Limited, registered in England, company number 785998, of Houndmills, Basingstoke, Hampshire RG21 6XS.

Palgrave Macmillan in the US is a division of St Martin's Press LLC, 175 Fifth Avenue, New York, NY 10010.

Palgrave Macmillan is the global academic imprint of the above companies and has companies and representatives throughout the world.

Palgrave® and Macmillan® are registered trademarks in the United States, the United Kingdom, Europe and other countries.

ISBN 978–1–4039–4739–0

This book is printed on paper suitable for recycling and made from fully managed and sustained forest sources. Logging, pulping and manufacturing processes are expected to conform to the environmental regulations of the country of origin.

A catalogue record for this book is available from the British Library.

A catalog record for this book is available from the Library of Congress.

10   9   8   7   6   5   4   3   2   1
21 20 19 18 17 16 15 14 13 12

Printed in China

Contents

Acknowledgements

I would like to thank all those that have made this book possible. To begin, all the contributors (i.e., Tessa Adams, Larry O'Carroll and Martin Stanton) for their tireless cooperation and creative production of exciting chapters. Catherine Gray and Esther Croom (from Palgrave Macmillan) for their patience and editorial guidance. Polona Curk for her assistance in editing the 'Introduction' of this book. All my friends and colleagues at RCTE, Roehampton University, who encouraged me to finish this book. I am also extremely grateful to the National Gallery (especially, Daragh Kenny) for giving us permission to reproduce Bronzino's 'An Allegory with Venus and Child', Titian's 'The Vendramin Family' and Velazquez's 'The Rokeby Venus' in the book and Dulwich Picture Gallery (especially, Fulvio Rubesa) for giving us permission to reproduce Poussin's 'Rinaldo and Armida'. Above all, I would like to thank my wife Maria whose love, support and understanding has helped to make everything I have accomplished possible.

Anastasios Gaitanidis

Notes on Contributors

Dr Anastasios Gaitanidis (editor) is a Senior Lecturer in Counselling Psychology, Counselling and Psychotherapy at Roehampton University, and an Associate Lecturer in Counselling at Goldsmiths College (University of London). He is also a Psychodynamic Counsellor/Psychotherapist in private practice. He is the Editor of *Narcissism – A Critical Reader* (2007) and he is currently co-editing the book *Authoring the Sublime* with Tessa Adams (Karnac).

Dr Tessa Adams is a Fellow of the Royal Society of Arts and Visiting Fellow of Goldsmiths College (University of London). She is an Art Theorist and practicing Psychoanalytic Psychotherapist, holding Professional Membership with both the Site of Contemporary Psychoanalysis and the Guild of Psychotherapists. She has published widely on psychoanalysis and contemporary art practice, and recently published a co-edited volume, *The Feminine Case: Jung, Aesthetics and Creative Process* with Karnac. She is also currently co-editing the book *Authoring the Sublime* with Anastasios Gaitanidis.

Larry O'Carroll is a Lecturer in Counselling at Canterbury College, Kent. He has published articles in journals including *Psychodynamic Counselling* and *Free Associations* and contributed a chapter in A. Gaitanidis's (ed.) *Narcissism – A Critical Reader* (Karnac). His research interests focus on the history of psychoanalytic theory, the work of Michel Foucault and the pragmatist philosophy of Richard Rorty.

Dr Martin Stanton is a psychoanalyst, writer and cultural critic. He is an Associate Research Fellow at the Institute of Continuing Education, University of Cambridge; Visiting Professor at Roehampton University; Consultant Staff Counsellor at Imperial College Healthcare NHS Trust; Employee Support Consultant at the University of Birmingham; and author of numerous books and articles including *Outside the Dream* (1982), *Sandor Ferenczi* (1990), and *Out of Order* (1998). Further details about his work, thinking, and creative life are available on his website, www.martinstanton.co.uk.

Introduction

Anastasios Gaitanidis

This book came out of a conversation with three colleagues – Tessa Adams, Larry O'Carroll and Martin Stanton (who have also contributed seven out of the nine chapters in this book) – about our work as psycho-analytic therapists and counsellors and, in particular, the many men we see in our practices. Our conversation led to many shared issues in the treatment of these men and the prevailing feeling that there is a need for critical thinking about the whole issue of masculinity as it has been taken up within psychoanalysis.

More specifically, we felt we were part of an academic culture which was heavily influenced by feminist, queer and postmodern theories that were bringing psychoanalysis into a world of constructed, fluid and multiply gendered possibilities. Yet what emerged in our conversa-tion was the virtual absence of the application of such critical thinking to the world of masculinity. For instance, in contrast to the excessive number of innovative theoretical and clinical examinations focusing on femininity, queer identity and psychoanalysis, new psychoanalytic theorizations of specific masculine issues were wanting. Thus we set out to both critically examine the already existing psychoanalytic accounts of masculinity and construct new ones.

One of the most dominant psychoanalytic accounts of the construction of masculinity is the 'classical' Freudian one which links the development of male identity to the little boy's Oedipal desire to possess the mother which brings him into conflict with his father. This conflict with the father is experienced as a threat to his penis (i.e., a threat of castration) as this is the area in his body that is directed towards gaining pleasure with his mother. This is primarily experienced in phantasy and perhaps reinforced by warnings about masturbation. The threat of castration is also reinforced by his conscious or unconscious realization that there

1

are 'castrated' beings in the world, that is, women. Under this threat, the little boy agrees to a compromise: he gives up his desire for his mother in return for a promise of becoming like the father and having a woman of his own when he is old enough. As part of this compromise, the little boy internalizes the father's prohibition against incest as an essential part of his superego. The function of the father, therefore, is to turn the little boy away from his mother and towards the world, to prevent the development of a closed incestuous unit.

This classical psychoanalytic theorization of the formation of male identity is severely criticized by Martin Stanton in his chapter 'Wrestling with Male(ness): Deconstructing the Virtual Macho World in Psychoanalysis and Culture'. More specifically, he looks at the enduring distortions surrounding the notion of the Oedipus complex, in which the original couple is taken to be pre-gendered (male/female) and copulating with a view to pre-determined procreation. Psychoanalysts working in this frame inevitably 'manage' the masculine through the son's (introjective or projective) identification with the penetrative procreative father, and failure to conform to this Oedipal idyll is duly pathologized.

Stanton argues rather for a notion of maleness which is negotiated by everyone as a part of their psychological development in relation to other(s). Maleness is a transference effect – like everything generated interpersonally – so is inevitably complex, and its ongoing elaborations will remain essentially unconscious (uninterpretable and residually unknown). For this reason, the male-effect inevitably subverts enclosure either in fixed gender discourse (essentialist masculinity) or in family-role stereotypes (i.e., mother/father). The progressive subversion of gender-family stereotypes by maleness engenders an ongoing living crisis of masculinity, which inevitably looms large in the consulting room and is mirrored in the transference.

Following Stanton's critique, Tessa Adams, in her chapter 'The Myth of Latency and the Construction of Boyhood', also criticizes the classical psychoanalytic account of the little boy's psychological development in which his attempt to possess the mother ends up in a life-long castration fear, a fear which is based precisely on 'the specificity of female genitalia that are seen to lack', and culminates in the boy's renunciation of his relationship with the mother. In effect, Adams writes, this process is characterized by the attempt to give up solicitude in favour of security and masculine potency, resulting in the social split between boyhood and manhood.

The 'dominant fiction of desire-less boyhood', held in check by the fear of castration, ends with puberty when the social imperative of the incest taboo relinquishes once again the reactivated feelings of the desire for the mother. Manhood, then, is based on significant losses, Adams argues, as boyhood identifications are linked to denial of maternal attachments, precisely the ones that are at the base of the girl's identifications with the mother.

In this respect, Adams partly follows Dinnerstein's (1976) and Chodorow's (1978) feminist account of male identity formation which firmly establishes the importance of women/mothers as central figures in emerging developmental schemes and later as subjective centres of desire and power. This response merges well with the rise of object relational approaches within psychoanalysis, which emphasize pre-Oedipal dynamics, consequently shifting focus and power from issues of castration to the mother–child dyad. More specifically, what this feminist account proposes is that, although children of both sexes must learn equally to distinguish self from other, and have fundamentally the same need for autonomy, to the extent that boys rest their very sexual identity on an opposition to what is both experienced and defined as feminine, the development of their gender identity is likely to emphasize on the process of separation. As boys, they must undergo a double 'disidentification' (Greenson, 1968) from mother – first for the establishment of a self-identity and second for the consolidation of a male gender identity. Further impetus is added to this process by the external cultural pressure on the young boy to establish a stereotypical masculinity based on absolute independence and autonomy. The cultural definitions of masculine as what can never present itself as feminine, and of autonomy as what can never be relaxed, conspire to reinforce the child's earliest associations of female with the pleasures and dangers of symbiotic fusion, and male with both the comfort and the loneliness of separateness. The boy's internal anxiety about both self and gender is here echoed by the cultural anxiety; together they can lead to attitudes of exaggerated and rigidified autonomy and masculinity which can – indeed which may be designed to – defend against that anxiety and the longing which generates it.

* * *

Yet, in this feminist/object relational account, fathers begin to recede from analytic view, appearing as secondary at best, and as absent and/or violent at worst. Fathers are now the ones who are lacking by virtue of their position outside of the mother-child dyad. Although it is helpful to see the adverse effects of patriarchy and male hegemony on society, it is important that fathers should be included in the theoretical discussions around masculinity.

For this reason, I argue in my chapter, 'Narcissism, Mourning and the 'Masculine' Drive' that the role of the Oedipal father should not be abandoned, but should be dialectically negated, that is, both negated and preserved. It is true that the role of the Oedipal father can be perceived as intrinsically violent since it imposes severe limitations on the son's ability to emotional connect with the (m)other and forces him to aspire to a form of identity which is based on separateness. However, by presenting his authority as a transient force that can be challenged, the father enables the son to mourn the loss of an internal ideal, omniscient and omnipotent paternal figure and identify with a more realistic, impermanent and potent one. The current disintegration of the function of the father signifies not only the end of patriarchal oppression, but also the end of the son's attempt to create a different, less violent relation with himself and others.

Following this line of thought, I propose in my next chapter 'The Phantom of the Primal Father' that the Lacanian account of the 'primal father' can be used to illustrate how the current disintegration of the father's authority leads men to subject themselves to an opaque Law (i.e., the Law of the dead primal father) which is alien and external to them. However, whereas the Lacanian account regards this alienation as a necessary constituent of the human condition and attempts to re-establish the power and significance of the father by transforming him into a phantom that possesses only a transcendent symbolic function (i.e., the Law of the – dead primal – Father), the Freudian one, in its insistence on the importance and continued relevance of certain concrete paternal qualities which have become outdated in the present, attempts to exorcise this phantom so as to allow men to struggle against their alienation and rethink the various aspects of their identity.

In her own attempt to emphasise the importance of the function of the father, Adams, in her chapter 'Locating the Male within the Psychoanalytic Tradition', turns to certain contemporary theorists, such as Jessica Benjamin (1995) and Thomas Domenici (in Domenici and Lesser, 1995). I have placed this chapter at the beginning of the book because it provides a critical overview of the majority of the old and recent psychoanalytic conceptualisations of masculinity and, therefore, sets the tone for the discussions that take place in the following chapters.

Benjamin and Domenici challenge the father's secondary role and suggest that the male child does not need to relinquish all that is 'other', including the maternal relationship, in order to identify with the male sex, but rather he can retain (even playfully and creatively) a multitude of identifications and forms of libidinal attachment. It could be said that these theorists in fact preserve Freud's original meaning of 'polymorphous perversity'. It is perhaps the playful character of these theories that can be contrasted to Chodorow's analysis that perceives the boy's positioning as necessarily involving the repudiation of maternal identifications, which together with the societal privileging of masculinity encourages the denial of maternal attachment.

This importance of multiple identifications in the formation of male identity is also emphasised by Frosh who in his two important books on the topic – *Sexual Difference: Masculinity and Psychoanalysis* (1994) and *After Words: The Personal in Gender, Culture and Psychotherapy* (2002) – argues that Benjamin's theory (together with Kristeva's (1983) notion of the 'father of individual prehistory') provides us with more productive ways of conceptualising the fluidity of male identity than the already existing psychoanalytic ones. For Frosh, the strength of Benjamin's position lies in its insistence on the significance of the concrete other (mother and/or father) for the infant boy, and its acknowledgement that there must be an element of mutuality in his primary relations to others, and hence greater substance to the principle of his independence than is allowed by its interpretation as the mere negation of his dependence upon the (m)other. The boy's recognition of and by the other is thus conceived as an inherently fluid relationship.

In many respects, Benjamin's approach is not unlike that of Jean Laplanche (1987). Both Benjamin and Laplanche emphasize the priority to the psychic life of the infant boy of his relations to the concrete other. They also both criticize classical psychoanalytic theory for its exclusive pre-occupation with the boy's intrapsychic situation, to the neglect of its actual relations with others. However, whereas Benjamin posits a primal relation of mutual recognition independent of the boy's relations to his internal representations, thereby introducing the other only at the cost of its separation from the realm of internal representations, Laplanche attempts to integrate the action of the concrete other and the intrapsychic domain of representation by separating off seduction from the primal fantasies with which it is associated by Freud, and understanding it, instead, as the logic of a primal 'communication situation' between adult and the infant boy: the implantation of the message of the other. For if the drive originates in messages (but not, of course, solely in verbal messages), then there is no initial or natural opposition between the instinctual and the intersubjective, or between the instinctual and cultural. Rather, this opposition must be understood as *produced* in the course of the boy's development, as the 'seduction' of the primal situation peels a sexual layer off the 'onion' of a self-preservative function which is simultaneously psychical and somatic.

However, Larry O'Carroll in his chapter 'On Men's Friendships with Other Men' wonders whether Laplanche's generalized notion of 'seduction' can function as a corrective to the psychoanalytic marginalization of male friendship (*philia*). He argues that the possibility that any human being could ever be 'emotionally literate', let alone sustain what certain psychoanalytic theorists call a 'mature relationship', is thrown into relief by Laplanche's re-configuration of psychoanalytic theory, especially vis-à-vis the birth of the ego and narcissism. When psychic differentiation begins with the birth of the ego and the closing down to the Other (sexuality) it sets in train, it remains inexplicable how mature hetero- and homosexual love, as well as desexualized friendship, can exist. In other words, since the appearance of the ego is to be conceived as effecting the closing down of the infant to the enigmatic sexual significations of the (m)other's unconscious activity, and narcissism consists in a primal repudiation of the (m)other, Laplanche's re-writing of psychoanalytic theory in terms of the infant's primal seduction by an already sexualized human world is unlikely to transform the marginalization of *philia* by psychoanalytic suspicion.

Having expressed his doubts regarding the adequacy and usefulness of the various psychoanalytic theorisations of male friendship (including Laplanche's), O'Carroll also wonders (in his chapter 'Deconstructing the Homosexual–Heterosexual Divide') whether psychoanalysis has any valuable insights to offer regarding male same-sex desire. He presents Stoller's and Sturbin's argument that psychoanalytic accounts of gay men are based on small samples of highly distressed gay men, ending up in the pathologization of male same-sex desire. This cannot be generalized to gay men as a whole, O'Carroll argues. The ancient Greeks furnish an example of how in another culture and time, a specific 'statistical deviance' can be normative, or even elitist, and that reproduction of our species is not at all endangered. In contrast, considering the history of psychoanalytic theoretical revisions not enough attention is paid to the similarities that 'any of the hetero- and homosexualities might have in common in respect of the quality of relationships they seek, and can sustain'.

What is also important for O'Carroll is the (Foucauldian) question: 'can we "create" our sexuality' as 'could it have been otherwise'? Because '"heterosexual" and "homosexual" are names', he argues, 'they may well disappear one day', perhaps through analysing the archive of history rather than treat it as an expression of 'general causality'. Progress might be slow, O'Carroll states, as psychoanalysis' powers are limited to therapeutic practice and dominant gender discourses still produce undesirable effects on us. But what is best about psychoanalysis is its ability to show that '"heterosexual" and "homosexual" are best understood as the rendezvous-points for complex psychical processes issuing in erotic object-choice'.

However, although psychoanalysis shows that men's fantasies, sexual practices, desires, longings, excitements, fears and anxieties are governed by complex psychic coordinates, it does not always pay attention to how certain social practices affect their psychic life. Psychoanalysis has always been about the interior life of individuals, yet considering how the exterior, social life of men affects their interior life can open the therapist up to unexpected surprises.

For this reason, Adams stresses a specific form of social practice to which men are constantly subjected, that is, social humiliation, which finds its expression in ritualistic practices such as 'beasting' as described at the beginning of her chapter 'The Fear of Male Humiliation'. Psychoanalytic theory describes shame, but not the shaming of the other, Adams complains. Perhaps this is so because hate is seen in classical psychoanalytic terms as an instinctual reaction and, thus, its social/relational origin is neglected, allowing for the existence of institutionalized forms of aggression. The social origin of humiliating practices needs to be taken into account and the relationship between primary aggression and social shaming should be analysed so as to be able to implement better preventative measures against them.

For instance, Adams emphasizes the need to prevent certain 'acceptable' humiliation practices from engendering masculine courage. In psychological terms, she contends, such 'training' practices rest 'on both the premise of narcissistic aggrandisement, on the one hand, and its disillusionment, on the other', establishing a conflict where the masculine ideal is to be forfeited and reinforced at the same time. In this 'perversion of power', intimidation becomes part of the dominant culture.

Following Adams' exploration of the impact of specific social practices (i.e., male humiliation) on men's sense of self-worth, O'Carroll reflects on psychoanalysis' ability to adequately understand and explain current social problems. In particular, what interests O'Carroll in his chapter 'Achieving Our Country: Ethnic Difference and White Men's Racism' is psychoanalysis' contribution to understanding white men's racism, although he points out at the very beginning that this is a complex socio-cultural and political problem that cannot be reduced only to an aspect of psychic processes. Moreover, psychoanalysis can only deal with individualised cases of a particular subject, but it should be noted that certain realities, like class relations and politics, have little to do with psychic processes; psychoanalysis' avoidance to account for particular historical/cultural condition represents a limit to its explanations of white men's racism.

Nonetheless, psychoanalysis has offered useful explanations to understanding racism. O'Carroll mentions early splitting into an idealized 'we' and a hated 'them', producing a fantasmatic inviolable boundary; it is the anxious fantasizing child that maintains this split imaginary. But this is not inevitable, O'Carroll argues. In fact, early omnipotent projection, splitting and idealization are attenuated during the development of human subjectivity, and the failure of this developmental process can be described as maligned with reality, as 'psychotic'. White men's racism, O'Carroll argues, is just that – primitive paranoid-schizoid functioning. If nothing else, then, psychoanalytic thought shows that racism is not inevitable as psychoanalysis holds that usually such functioning is transformed in the course of psychological development. This shows, O'Carroll points out, that although in-group/out-group relations will always exist, racism is not an inevitable consequence of white men's socialisation and, thus, a tolerant socio-political environment is possible.

Apart from Adams' and O'Carroll's investigation of the social practices of humiliation and racist attitudes that haunt the construction of masculine identity, all four contributors in this book equally recognize and examine the enormous impact that recent social changes have had on the lives of men. More specifically, they realise that most men are currently undergoing an identity crisis and, as this crisis intensifies, they feel the need to cling to ideas of manhood which no longer serve them well and by which they are trapped. As the present society forces them to abandon their 'traditional' modes of subjectification without promoting any new and/or viable ones, a significant number of men seem to embark on a vain attempt to reconstitute a failing sense of masculinity. All four contributors, therefore, feel the need to criticise the existing cultural landscape which compels men to aspire to outdated models of masculinity. I hope that the book in its totality will invite men to join our collective endeavour to criticise the existing psychoanalytic and cultural assumptions regarding the formation of male identities and encourage them to find the strength to create new ones.

1
Locating the Male within the Psychoanalytic Tradition

Tessa Adams

This chapter addresses the ways in which the adult male is conceived psychoanalytically with reference to the questions that are raised by developmental theory from various accepted perspectives. Attention is given to the contrast between paternal and maternal significations and the positioning of the father in relation to them.

Freud and Lacan: The primacy of the phallus

Clearly, the focus on the potency of maleness, in psychoanalytic terms, owes much to Freud's attention to the significance of the male body part (the penis) and the fear of castration. Freud casts the infant boy as protective of this attribute in the face of the infant girl's lack of it. The feminist argument against Freud refers to his apparent inability to offer a symmetrical account of the Oedipal crisis for the infant girl in contrast to his concentration on the infantile sexual neurosis of the infant boy which claims that the infant boy in the discovery of his genital encounters desire and in seeking gratification is deterred by the fear of castration. In contrast, the infant girl is seen to experience neither the joy of genital discovery nor the fear of its demise, since she sees herself as a castrated subject through the lack of this crucial body part. Thus the drama of genital discovery is located as primarily the project for the male infant with the annexing of the female genitalia as a failure to provide. Freud furthers this contrast by indicating that the infant can have no awareness of the womb, regarding instead the production of babies as emitting from the anus.

Moreover, Freud's assertion that the libido is essentially masculine (from which the feminine diverges) means that the psychical development of the girl is initially seen to be identical with that of the boy, only to be differentiated later (for a comprehensive discussion of Freud's characterization of libido as masculine, see Gaitanidis's 'Narcissism, Mourning and the "Masculine" Drive', Chapter 4 in this book). Thus it can be argued that this positioning of the feminine renders the masculine paradigmatic (this argument is developed more extensively in 'The Myth of Latency and the Construction of Boyhood, Chapter 3 in this book). Yet Freud (1926) demonstrates a certain unrest in his asymmetrical analysis by indicating that, for him, the feminine is mysterious by claiming it to be a 'dark continent' (p. 212). Furthermore, his concern is evidenced by statements such as, 'Psychoanalysis does not try to describe what a woman is – that would be a task it could scarcely perform – but sets out about enquiring how she comes into being, how a woman develops out of a child with a bisexual disposition' (Freud, 1933, p. 116).

One of the striking influences of the latter part of the twentieth century is the attention to the Lacanian thesis in respect to the phallus as the primary signifier of the Western economy. This privileging of the phallus is derived from Lacan's assumption that language as law pertains to the father; in his claim that the Name of the Father (*Le Nom-du-Pere*) through its privileging of the phallus as a primary signifier provides a guarantee through which language can signify – that is, produce meaning. Evans (1996) explains this bias in the following way: 'Lacan argues that "there is no symbolisation of woman's sex as such" since there is no feminine equivalent to the "highly prevalent symbol" provided by the phallus' (p. 220). The question that arises here is why is it seen to be appropriate to hamper the male with so much social/cultural/linguistic responsibility where the symbolic necessity of the primacy of the phallus attributes maleness with the inscription of the constraints of the law?

If it is agreed that Freud and Lacan hold the masculine as paradigmatic and treat the feminine as fugitive in the context of the primacy of the masculine position, it could appear that the Genesis account of the dominance of Adam has psychoanalytically taken root. Yet this gendered dissymmetry problematizes either party, and while there has been considerable feminist debate to offer challenge, it is significant that masculine concerns seem to be under-represented. That is to say, while much psychoanalytic writing (such as the works of Karen Horney and Juliette Mitchell) has sought to revise what is seen to be the patriarchal bias in Freud's writing (in respect of the infantile sexual neurosis), when the impact on the male is considered, there appears to be a lack of discussion. Arguably, a problematic exists (for the male) in claims that situate the male body part (i.e., the phallus) as symbolically framing desire.

Klein, Kristeva and Winnicott: The primacy of the maternal realm

In the light of Freud's passive positioning of the feminine, it is hardly surprising that Melanie Klein saw fit to lay emphasis on the dynamic of the maternal. While Freud accepts the mother as the child's first love object, he focuses on the intervention of the father (and the threat of castration) as the means by which desire for the mother is relinquished. In this exchange, identification with the father furnishes the internalization of prohibition from which position the Oedipal crisis is resolved. However, it is clear that Klein's placing of the father is of a different order in that she not only locates the drama of the mother–baby relationship in terms of the infant's pre-Oedipal experience but offers an analysis as to how the father is pre-Oedipally encountered, in phantasy. For Klein, the mother's body (in early infancy) becomes so privileged in part-object terms that the presence of the father is subjected to secondary function. That is to say, while Klein dwells on the infant's phantasies that directly meet the absence and presence of the mother's body (perceived as the providing or rejecting breast) the father's body is virtually cast as an aspect of the mother. What this means is that Klein claims that in the early months the father is phantasized as incorporated within the mother's body (as either penis or the whole body) to become subjected to attack. The following passage from *Envy and Gratitude* (1946–63) makes this clear:

> According to the child's earliest phantasies (or 'sexual theories') of parental coitus, the father's penis (or his whole body) becomes incorporated in the mother during the act. Thus the child's sadistic attacks have for their object both father and mother, who are in phantasy bitten, torn cut or stamped to bits.
>
> (Klein, 1946–63, p. 219)

Klein indicates that within this early period of infancy gender specificity is not established and proposes that the infant conceives a 'maternal penis … concealed inside the vagina' (Klein, 1923, p. 69). Further, Klein frames this initial experience of the presence of the father as persecutory in serving the phantasy of a 'combined parental figure' (for an extensive critique of Klein's notion of the 'combined parental couple', see O'Carroll's 'Deconstructing the Homosexual-Heterosexual Divide', Chapter 7 in this book). What this means is that the infant's early encounter with the father fails to locate him as a subject of provision, since he is primarily located as an object of threat. What is interesting, though, is that Klein suggests that the dynamic of this early persecutory positioning of the father is seen later to give way to a relational exchange through the establishment of the Depressive Position. Klein proposes that during this position (instigated at the onset of weaning) the infant learns to perceive 'whole' objects and, from this perspective, the father is seen as compensatory, since her claim is that the child turns to the father in order to mitigate the disappointment with the mother. This suggests that during the process of the infant's depressive struggle, the father's presence becomes important as both the means of a new-found potential of loving engagement and as the agency of autonomy.

It could be argued that the problematic for the male, in Klein's analysis, is that the early experience of the infant (although defined as the object of phantasy) is seen to be subsumed by the infant's recourse to envious attacks towards the mother which leave the male symbolically significant, yet challenging. Furthermore, Klein appears to relegate the masculine, at best, to a compensatory positioning within the developmental paradigm of early infant experience, a reaction perhaps to Freud's exemplification of the penis as the primary signifier of Oedipal resolution.

What is interesting, however, is that Klein's indication of the infant's phantasmic installation of the 'maternal penis' virtually anticipates the French psychoanalyst Julia Kristeva who, in her book *Desire in Language* (1980), proposes that in early infancy there is a need to conceive of the 'phallic mother'. Kristeva's work draws from object relations theory, on the one hand, and Lacanian theses, on the other. Simply put, Kristeva's concern is that when the infant moves from the state of rev-erie (*jouissance*) of the symbiotic encounter which frames the maternal universe, before the fracture of signification – law, language, sign and syntax – pertaining to both the symbolic father and the recognition of the actual father, a compensatory fiction is envisaged, namely, that of the 'phallic mother'. This phantasy provides the infant with the illusion that the mother needs no other and thereby is believed to be totally available without reserve. The father in this case, as with Klein, is seen to disrupt. However, while Kristeva accepts that there is a non-disruptive, identificatory relationship with the father at this stage (that of the father of one's own individual pre-history), his presence is nevertheless seen as more profoundly one of rupture since her claim is that the infant, in finding language (law), is compelled to eschew the maternal universe from consciousness in order to commit to the socialization of the group. Significantly, Kristeva casts this shift from the mother as virtually a per-manent loss in stating that 'Language as symbolic function constitutes itself at the cost of repressing instinctual drive and continuous relation to mother' (Kristeva, 1980, p. 136). That is to say, it is Kristeva's claim that the patriarchal discourse eclipses the maternal realm rendering the latter permanently subversive. Yet, Kristeva suggests a level of mitigation in that the relegation of the maternal realm is compensated by the prospect of its reinstatement that engenders a bid for recognition – a breaking through the constraints of patriarchal dominance – by means of creative processes as exemplified by the poetic text.

However, although Kristeva offers a level of retrieval of the maternal through unconscious means, it is clear that the paternal discourse is seen to be prohibitive in terms of the infant's original symbiotic relation to the mother. Arguably, the recognition of the primary signifier (i.e., the phallus) is seen to rob and yet paradoxically provide. For, although the paternal function challenges the infant's maternal relationship, it ensures the 'social-symbolic-linguistic contract with the group' (Kristeva, 1980, p. 136). It could be suggested that Kristeva's positioning offers the male child a daunting legacy since the symbolic phallus, in seeming to dominate discourse, is also the body part that will eventually exemplify maleness in potency.

Furthermore, Kristeva has also drawn inspiration from Winnicott and it is significant that the latter, by and large, locates the positioning of the father in terms of social provision. As a paediatrician, Winnicott's attention was to the well-being of a child primarily in terms of maternal care, which led him to analyse the infant's psychological development from the early mother–baby symbiotic union towards developing autonomy. The role of the father, or the male carer, in his view, is one of a facilitator, both in terms of support and provision and in terms of the child's entry to the world. Winnicott places significant emphasis on pre-natal experience, which he claims initiates maternal preoccupation. In the last months of pregnancy, he states, the father becomes the 'protective agent who frees the mother to devote herself to the baby' (Wiinicott in Davis and Wallbridge, 1981, p. 134). The term Winnicott uses to encapsulate this paternal role implies a 'canopy', since he speaks of the father offering a 'protective covering' that is essential to the infant's welfare. Furthermore, Winnicott warns that this 'canopy' is critical by suggesting that illnesses of childbirth can 'to some extent be brought about by the failure of this protective covering' (ibid.). The implication here is that for Winnicott the male parent is seen to be objectified with a responsibility that is both distant and enduring. In a way similar to Klein's, Winnicott places the father as mitigating the disillusionment that arises from the infant's developing awareness that the mother inevitably will be seen to fail the ideal. Furthermore, Winnicott equally suggests that the child's aggression can be directed towards the father, although from a different perspective. Klein sees the aggression as deriving from the phantasies that locate the father's place within the mother's body, while Winnicott identifies aggression towards the father as based upon the infant perceiving the father as 'other' and belonging to the outside world. Winnicott's claim is that the child (in conceiving the father as the 'third term') seeks the opportunity to split hate from love, at which time hatred for the mother can be safely projected onto the enduring presence of the father. However, although Winnicott also casts the father as facilitator (in ensuring that the child can achieve autonomy from the mother) in this position, he primarily sees the father as the person who can be 'kicked against'.

Questioning the psychoanalytic positioning of the male

A question that can be raised here is, whether or not, psychoanalysis is able to privilege the male in terms other than that of provision and/or prohibition. In other words, where does the nurturing male reside if not seen in compensatory terms? As we have seen, Freud's purpose for the male is primarily as the agent of socialization since identification (for the male child) is framed as the libidinal solution that engenders the dissolution of the Oedipal conflict. Kristeva, following Lacan, advocates male intervention as that which disrupts the child's symbiosis with the mother, thereby offering the prospect of a greater gain, namely, the subject's contract with the group. In the case of Klein, the male is proposed as interlocutrix (in phantasy) embraced within the mother's body, offering a challenge to sublime union, in the first instance, the progress of which will eventually serve the infant in terms of mitigating the loss of the ideal (self/mother/union). Thus, the infant, in perceiving the mother as the 'whole object', can bear the loss since the good (providing) and bad (depriving) breast can no longer be separated. In contrast to the attention to the internal imagos of the male that Freud, followed by Klein, appears to prioritize, Winnicott can be seen to be effecting the 'Knight's move'. For the shift, in Winnicott's terms, resonates in releasing the concern from the intra-psychic positioning of the male to the actual realities of child rearing. What this means is that Winnicott's thesis is possibly the most embracing evaluation of the positioning of the male in that he locates the male as both actual and symbolic facilitator in providing the 'protective covering' on which the mother's early nurturing of an infant will depend. In other words, Winnicott's thesis claims that the father enables both the symbiotic care that tempers the stresses and strains of the mother's earliest encounter, on the one hand, and the gaurdianship on which emerging adulthood will depend, on the other. Fundamental to Winnicott's view is the recognition of a level of objectivity in the father–child relationship (due to the father appearing as other) that institutes the means by which the child authenticates outside relationships.

It could be argued that, in the main, these descriptions of the role of the father present us with a dilemma, since the psychoanalytic encounter with the male is seen to be crucial to infant development, yet, in many ways, of secondary function. This, of course, is in keeping with the view that intra-utero life is more than a simple biological dynamic. Thus, as these theories suggest that the primary need of the infant is for maternal validation (principally the experience of the benevolent breast), they relegate the position of the male as primarily critical in the processing of the reality of experience. As we have seen, in Lacanian terms, the male is the carrier of the primary signifier – the phallus – which establishes Law and syntax. In Winnicottian terms, the male is conceived as both protector and the facilitator of socialization. In Freudian terms, the male is seen as competitor and the object of identification, the means by which primitive desire is transformed (sublimated) in order to serve social aims.

Benjamin, Domenici, Chodorow and Richards: Repositioning the male

Marie Maguire in her paper 'The Website "Girl": Contemporary Theories about Male "Femininity"' (2005) alludes to the core of this problem when she claims that the position of the male is significantly unresolved. Speaking of the father, she implies that the development of post-Freudian theory has subjected the actual presence of the father to a symbolic social referent:

> Despite attempts to rehabilitate the father in much contemporary [psychoanalytic] theory he remains a shadowy figure. He is still secondary to the mother and does not intervene as a powerful sexual presence, a representative of authority and as culture, as in Freud's theory. Yet recognition of the role of the (symbolic) father is vital for understanding how patriarchal structures reproduce themselves even when parents make a conscious effort to avoid reinforcing them.
>
> (Maguire, 2005, p. 15)

But we can ask if this 'secondary' position is that which the male is bound to take – appearing as provider that is crucial to the infant's socialization, yet seemingly expendable. Jessica Benjamin's concern is that it is not necessary for the boy to be so psychologically differentiated. Rather, for Benjamin, the male child can be seen (in developing the sense of belonging to one sex) as neither in need of relinquishing all that is 'other' nor drawn into an essential forfeiting of a potential range of identifications (Benjamin, 1995). That is to say, Benjamin offers a challenge to propositions that seemingly wrench the boy child from maternal relationship and identifications (in classical Freudian terms) by suggesting a level of flexibility in the forms of libidinal attachment that developing boyhood can experience.

This bid for a greater flexibility in understanding the position of the male is also borne out by Thomas Domenici who, in his co-edited book *Disorientating Sexuality* (Domenici and Lesser, 1995), suggests that where a boy has an original attachment to both the father and the mother, there is the opportunity to 'play' with different co-existing desires and gendered identities. This position is clearly in keeping with Freud's assumption of 'polymorphous perversity' that characterizes the desires of early infancy. Yet, in suggesting the capacity for the adoption of differing identities, Domenici implies that Oedipal neurosis is redundant, since Domenici's view of playful experimentation with gendered identity suggests that, in recognizing choice, we can secure a less unconscious relationship with desire. Both Domenici and Benjamin indicate the potential to creatively integrate same and opposite sex characteristics. However, their position is in direct contrast to Chodorow (1994) who situates the positioning of the boy, as of necessity, intent upon the repudiation of maternal relationship and thereby maternal identifications. Chodorow proposes that the societal privileging of masculinity (in which male superiority is applauded) engenders boyhood identifications that leave the male subject caught up in a web of denial of maternal attachment. As she expressed it:

> The subjective gendering of masculine love is not neutral. Subjective gendering for men means that such love defines itself negatively in relation to the mother as well as in terms of positive love attachment ... insistent masculine superiority and asymmetry in [hetero]sexuality indicate a defensive construction.
>
> (Chodorow, 1994, p. 84)

Thus, there is a debate still to be exercised as to whether, or not, a more flexible positioning of the masculine is possible, since the social construction of gender has been dominated by the legacy of male superiority. Yet, without this flexibility the father, as already mentioned, is located as generating the manifestation of process rather than relationship as he is seen as primarily the agent of prohibition and the provider of reality. As Richards emphasizes in her co-edited book *Fathers, Families and the Outside World* (Richards with Wilce, 1997), the entry of the father denotes sexual difference which, of necessity, ensures the process of socialization. Introducing her edited text that is listed under the remit of 'Winnicottian Studies', Richards cites Eagleton (1985) whose support of the Freudian paradigm (in terms of differentiation) is stated in the following way:

> For the drama of the Oedipus complex to come about at all, the child must ... have become dimly aware of sexual difference. It is the entry of the father which signifies this 'sexual difference'. ... It is only by accepting the necessity of sexual difference, of distinct sexual roles, that the child, who has been previously unaware of such problems, can become properly 'socialised'.
>
> (Eagleton, 1985, pp. 165–6)

Significantly the father is described as 'entering' as if he has not been part of the original process of conception. He appears to be a stranger who 'brings something in' that is crucial but disrupting. Clearly carrying a baby in pregnancy can appear as if the child is the possession of the mother, yet the potentiality and foundation of life derives equally from the partnership that created it. Thus, there seems to be a rift between the essential role that the male performs in the creation of pregnancy and the widespread belief that he is fundamentally external to it. This is no more evident than in case of the phenomenon of 'sperm banks'. Even the term 'bank' suggests a product of the male that has become a commodity, and in doing so, removes both the identity of the donor and the legacy of contribution. Thus it is as if the stuff of life from the male is considered to be in question since, on the one hand, it is implied to be potentially highly relevant, while, on the other, virtually expendable. What is interesting is that contemporary concerns as to the presence of the father have recently instigated certain legislation in order to ensure that the 'free marketing' of sperm is brought to a halt. Equally, the revisioning of original parenthood (in the case of adoption) has meant that full records are required in order that fathers can be located with the purpose of ensuring that the genetic 'footprint' of all individuals has the potential of being traced. It seems that it has been a long wait for fatherhood (in all of its vicissitudes) to dare to address these and other critical concerns for the male.

Jung: The male and the contra-sexual archetypes

If we consider Jung's thesis of the contra-sexual archetypes (*Anima* and *Animus*) it could be argued that he attempts to situate the masculine and feminine functions as virtually interchangeable. In his privileging of the 'feminine' of the male as unconscious experience, Jung implies that there is a distinct desire and capacity in men to fulfil the demands of their internal feminine 'nature' and (by implication) nurturing roles. Equally, Jung's thesis offers the dynamic of the unconscious 'masculine' influencing women through manifesting certain 'masculine' capacities such as discrimination. What is evident is that Jung appears to both revise the stereotype, on the one hand, while appearing to reinforce it, on the other. In the first place, an analysis of the psyche that embraces contra-sexual potential to a certain extent can be seen as radical. Yet Jung's adherence to the thesis of oppositional dispositions in respect of masculine and feminine attributes reproduces a conventional problematic. That is to say, Jung argues that the male is dominated by the masculine quality of 'Logos', while conversely, the female is dominated by the feminine quality of 'Eros'. This is in keeping with Jung's (1955–6) statement that 'The opposites are the ineradicable and indispensable pre-conditions of all psychic life' (p. 170). Thus, the interiority of the anima, in the case of the male, mitigates logos, and equally women (unconsciously) meet the potential (discrimination) of logos which modifies eros.

It could be argued that Jung is unequivocal in his gendered attribution of that which is seen to predispose maleness. In the first instance, the male is cast as 'active' in opposition to the 'passivity' of the female. This is followed by a listing of characteristics that carve out maleness, namely, 'rationality' and 'discrimination', in opposition to female 'intuition' and 'connectedness'. And while Jung states that his system of defining masculine and feminine qualities (under the aegis of logos and eros respectively) are basically 'conceptual aids', he seems clear in his position by asserting that 'Woman's [consciousness] is characterised more by the connective quality of eros than by the discrimination and cognition associated with logos' and "eros, the function of relationship, is usually less developed" in men' (Jung, 1959, p. 14). Thus, on the one hand, Jung anticipates the positioning of male attributes that can be associated with the patriarchal law, while, on the other, the unconscious signification of the anima seemingly offers the male a plethora of feminine qualities. As the following passage confirms:

> Every mother and every beloved is forced to become the carrier and embodiment of this omnipresent and ageless image, which corresponds to the deepest reality in man. It belongs to him, this perilous image of Woman; she stands for loyalty which in the interest of life he must sometimes forgo; she is the much needed compensation for the risks, struggles, sacrifices that all end in disappointment; she is the solace for all bitterness of life. ... This image is 'My Lady Soul' as Spitteler called her. I have suggested instead the term 'anima', as indicating something specific, for which the expression 'soul' is too general and too vague. The empirical reality summed up under the concept of the anima forms an extremely dramatic content of the unconscious.
>
> (Jung, 1959, p. 13)

It can be seen that Jung's ambition is for the androgyny of archetypal influence (which in the case of the male indicates an unconscious access to the deepening influence of the feminine principle – anima), to privilege maleness with the qualities of nurturing. Furthermore, when the unconscious dynamic of the animus is considered, Jung implies a far less advantage for women in meeting the masculine principle. It is as if the qualities of the masculine are overshadowed by the feminine. In addition, it is noticeable that Jung's principle of the influence of the Mother Archetype far outweighs his references to the father. Thus again the male is relegated in the following ways: first, in terms of the animus indicating a problematic in Jung's positioning of the contrasexual archetype for women which is in direct contrast to the bounty of the trope of the feminine that Jung indicates is available to the male through accessing the unconscious dynamic of the anima; and, second, in terms of the significance of the Mother Archetype, which Jung clearly sees as fundamentally more powerful than the paternal counterpart when he states:

> If I were a philosopher of platonic strain, I would say: somewhere, in 'a place beyond the skies', there is a prototype of or primordial image of the mother that is pre-existent and supraordinate to all the phenomena in which the 'maternal', in the broadest sense of the term, is manifest.
>
> (Jung, 1954, p. 75)

The problem here is not that Jung simply envisages a trajectory of the maternal so imbued. Rather, it is that the paternal archetype is left wanting. When considering the prospect for the male to identify with the legacy of archetypal masculinity, we find that Jung simply offers the 'Hero' and the 'Senex', both of whom are far less powerfully conceived. It could be argued that in respect of these iconographic expressions of maleness, Jung has appropriated the literal positioning of the male in terms of seeking courage at the start of life and wisdom towards its ending, while the Mother Archetype is conceived as enduring through time.

Conclusion

Finally, is it possible to summarize where, within the theoretical underpinning of psychodynamic process, the male is situated? We can conclude that, as already mentioned, largely, the position of the male is seen in terms of social provision and prohibition. According to Jung, maleness unconsciously carries the potency of the feminine since the male is viewed as being influenced by the anima (which refers to the Maternal Archetype) and yet is unable to partake of it. Furthermore, in privileging the Maternal Archetype Jung locates the relational capacity of the male that is seen to be the feminine mitigation of the non-relational masculine logos. In the case of contemporary theorists like Benjamin and Domenici, the male is seen to be less constrained. For this is a position that offers the male the opportunity to both 'play' with desire and gender identification and thereby relinquish his rigid masculine function which is the product of an unquestionable adherence to the Lacanian Law of the Father. Perhaps, psychoanalysis is troubled by the prospect of creative masculinity since the societal positioning of the male, in Freudian and Lacanian terms, speaks of the threat of castration, provoking an attempt to symbolize the male body part as both penis and phallus, which leaves the relational dynamic of maleness unaddressed. In contrast, Klein is equally concerned to privilege the breast in much the same fashion and thereby elaborate the infant's literal bid for sustenance as a phantasmic drama of acceptance and repudiation. In respect to Kristeva and Winnicott, who locate the father as the agency of social integration, the emphasis is laid on the sublime of maternal engagement. Kristeva speaks of maternal *jouissance* while Winnicott advocates a symbiotic maternal reverie casting the father's responsibility as that of the 'facilitating environment'. In each of these cases it can be suggested that the maternal relationship is deemed as virtually transcendent with the implication that the male (as the purveyor of reality) heralds loss and prohibition.

Thus the infant is seen to internalize the axiom of asymmetry in which the maternal is largely represented as relational and the paternal as productive. This, of course, is in keeping with the social construction of gender roles which, although in contemporary terms demonstrates the prospect of a degree of revision, subscribes to the view that mothers are more intuitively capable of securing a nurturing relationship.

2

Wrestling with Male(ness): Deconstructing the Virtual Macho World in Psychoanalysis and Culture

Martin Stanton

Masculinity and maleness

This chapter will focus on maleness – the effects that variously produce the sense of being male – rather than masculinity. I will argue that masculinity is a cumbersome imminently redundant concept that is mostly used to shore up reactionary essentialist projects promoting 'the real man' – a character anchored in fixed immutable masculine psychological features (including set male ways of thinking). In contrast, maleness highlights the interpersonal interactive production of being male. Maleness is a complex effect within a system that mixes ready-made and spontaneously improvised productions of performing male, with the promotion of the repressed and unconscious dynamics underlying being male – in particular, the complex elaborative workings and re-workings in transference of all those things from the other that provoke feeling/being male. In short, maleness is not founded in some 'real male nature' (masculinity), but it is variously produced in transference between any human subjects (however gendered), and follows the specific figurative process of that transference. It variously amalgamates, edits or evacuates bits of male into a composite maleness.

So – to begin – why consign the concept of masculinity to the scrapheap? Masculinity is so highly fraught a concept in contemporary life because it draws on two distinct discursive orders, which are both potentially mutually exclusive, and always in conflict: first of all, masculinity draws on gender, and the standard bifurcation of humans into male and female, based on anatomical differences perceived in sexual maturation; and secondly, masculinity is elaborated around set social positions, functions, exchanges and roles, which are defined both within trans-generational group process (the configuration of (grand)fathers and sons in the family), and within an on-going cultural (re)production of maleness (including its media (re)construction as a spectacle, with all marketing, hype and trash generated therein).

Critical attempts to define masculinity tend therefore to be reductive of one discursive order to the other – so generate their own explanatory *'contusions'* from the f(r)iction between the gender/culture narratives imposed by a fixed conception of masculine nature ('psychic contusion' is a term I have introduced to describe the internal psychological process of trauma as it configures the intra-psychic reverberations that follow a blow – reverberations which connect trauma-points (or *contundors*) to their on-going bruise-like elaborations (Stanton, 1997, pp. 79ff; & Stanton, 1993)). Such critical attempts either collapse into biological essentialism – where the distinctive physical attributes of the male (possession of male genitals or physical size and strength) are taken automatically to mark out (innate) psychological characteristics and implicit social function (ethics) for masculinity – notably in indicating a predisposition for power/aggression to protect the family and its laws in the position of either (patriarchal) judge or (dutiful son) warrior. Or conversely critical attempts to define masculinity collapse into the infinite regress of cultural relativism – in which the masculine is seen to be shaped by a set of current discourses in which the subject is immersed (or allowed to buy in) into prominent tropes that enable the male (to be assertive, competitive, powerful etc.), and also set infinitely free to mix (like some DJ at the turntables) a new essential male form (the new man).

Nowhere are the contusive dynamics – and explanatory contusions – involved in accounting for masculinity more visible than in critical forays into male sexuality. The undisputed *tour de force* here must be the 'biologising off-trackness' (*le fourvoiement biologisant*) of Freud's theory of masculine sexuality (Laplanche, 2001) in which Freud tries to cross-map specific family position (around the (law of) father) with sexual identity/orientation (through the Oedipus complex). He equally tries to force-syncretise biological with psycho-sexual maturation processes, generating a phallo-privileged sexual developmental dynamic in which the father marks out the presence/absence and lack/removal of the penis. The contusive distortion imposed by this cross-mapping has generated its own specific theoretical hot spots/sore points – not least around the politics of lack – in particular around the castration complex, penis envy, and the lack subsequently generated in knowing what women innately desire (sexually), supposedly from the male.

So – given such resonant amputations within reductive elaborations of masculinity – let us now return to the concept of maleness. What might enable the concept of maleness to be more effective in incorpo-rating the contusions generated around being/performing male than the concept of masculinity? First of all, it enables exploration of the quality of being/performing male as an effect generated in all relations with others (transference), as opposed to some internally installed fixed essence exclusive to male-gendered subjects. As a transference effect, the quality of being/performing male also eludes any pre-formed inscription into sexual nature – in particular into fixed body-sites whose special lure is taken to derive exclusively from the anatomical distinction between the sexes. In contemporary culture, the penis has been so visibly and exploitatively overcharged with having to signify some essential and distinctive male nature (masculinity) that its chronic de-tumescence (symbolic impoverishment) is hardly surprising. It is not surprising either that the quality of being/performing male has overflowed elsewhere, to body sites/physical sensations not exclusively defined by anatomical difference or gender (such as specific genital/sexual function)

The contusive origins of maleness

Freud's major breakthrough in understanding the emergence and develop-ment of sexual experience was to uncover a primary structure – a primal scene – in which the child is an observer of the adult sexual world and tries to make sense of it in the limited terms available. Central therefore in the child's entry into sexuality was the theory s/he produced to explain what was seen and experienced. This theory was an amalgam of current fictional accounts of the origin of the species – such as the stork flight to deliver the baby – in which the child found itself immersed, and the specific emotional resonances generated by the primal scene. The child could be terrified – believing, for example, that lovers locked in intercourse were in serious conflict or battle – or curious or intrigued (left wanting to know more) – if the scene entailed muffled sounds heard through a wall. In all cases, for Freud, the child's theory was fictional – it incorporated both the child's own imaginative elaborations and chunks of ambient popular fiction – and it was emotionally integrative – it uniquely and individually configured the impact and ongoing resonances of the scene on the child's world. As the individual subsequently and progressively enters the (adult) sexual world, the theory undergoes substantial revisions, supposedly to enable the individual to integrate their sexual drives/productions into the set family frame (the Oedipus complex). Nonetheless, the basic structure of the theory remains central to sexual experience. It negotiates the contrapuntal dynamics of the individual's creative erotic output against the input of the otherness of sexual desire – or all that is mutually communicated (wanted and (re)acted upon) and enmeshed in ready-made and commoditized narratives about (male/female) intercourse. For Freud, this theory displays an unconscious core which is rooted in the primal scene. As it is unconscious, it is unknowable/unknown, but its effects emerge and resonate with each sexual return/repetition, which in turn are driven by all that remains enigmatic (un-interpretable) in desire for (an) other.

For Freud, these fictional elaborations cluster around *imagos* (a term which was originally introduced by Jung in 1912), or the primary immutable images rooted in the fissures (interpretative lack) in the primal scene. Not surprisingly, Freudian imagos cluster principally around the distinct otherness of mother and father (paternal and maternal imagos), but subsequent theoretical elaborations of the imago (in particular Ferenczi, Klein, Balint, Lacan and Laplanche) focus rather on their pre-ego (non-symbolized) otherness. Imagos here are mapped prior to the syncretic impact of family narratives, that is, directly onto pre-ego viscerally charged (cathected) body-sites engaged by the other. On this level, imagos trap the unprocessed elements of the interpersonal exchange (transference) in variously elaborated and affect-laden scenes. Above all, these imagos articulate – hence capture – the flux and vicissitudes of the engagement with the other (Stanton, 1998). The imago is driven by otherness – their body-sites are fragmented (imagos of the fragmented body/*imagos du corps morcele* (Lacan, 1936)) in reflection of the projective/introjective counter-thrust, with all its aggressive/painful sado/masochistic potential. So the very structure of the imago is an amalgam of more and less elaborated (symbolized/narrated) material generated by interpersonal exchange (transference), in which the rifts (non-translatable bits) between the components are trapped in an affect (viscerally charged site).

How then does maleness emerge and constellate within a primal scene? What is the role (theatrical function) of imagos in this? First and foremost, male(ness) is an effect in an interpersonal exchange (transference), in which the complex interaction of input and output generates an amalgam of ambient raw (unprocessed) and set (recipe) components. The effect (of being/performing) male is not fixed – it shifts and evolves in reaction to the otherness generated in the scene – and it remains essentially unconscious, as all that binds the various components of the amalgam male residually resist translation/symbolization – which in turn inevitably re-cycles desire (to know /unlock the enigma/ theorize) towards the other. In this literal sense, the imagos which articulate male(ness) are not subjectively rooted in body(sites) – such as the penis – but in the on-going process of interaction with other(ness) in which male amalgamates various raw and fixed elements. This process itself incorporates both relatedness – in touch(ness) with other(ness) – and residually non-assimilated (unconscious) elements that produce ongoing psychic contusions (generating various effects amalgamating excitement/pleasure or pain/conflict).

Male imagos

Male imagos emerge in the battle between set cultural narratives (that construct normal family life), and the on-going affect-driven charge produced in relations with the other. They emerge at the stalling-points or stand-offs in the cognitive enmeshment (the communicative transparency) of the relationship (Lagache, 1963; Lacan, 1968) – notably when set social narratives (taboos) are short-circuited by the charge generated by contact with the other; or when taboos – or some deflating version of reality – collapse the on-going affective exchange (intercourse). In both cases, the imago will freeze – or fix the affect – at the point in the narrative where the intercourse (knowledge/theory of the other) stalled. This point can either be a pre-formed item or feature of a given cultural narrative that is charged with some non-translatable or enigmatic affect (such as loss, lack or collapse); or indeed the sensorial body (sensitivity/numbness) or psycho-physiological site (panic/anxiety) that immediately preceded (or triggered) the stalling.

Male imagos encapsulate a transference relationship in which being male obtrudes in the communicative flow between people, then generates contusion in the on-going cognitive and sensorial processes involved. So male imagos both concretely capture and configure relationship with and between other(s) – most visibly through fixed and on-going contact between body-sites (mouth, anus, penis, vagina) – as well as generate specific affects that supplement the sense of being male. The resultant contusion excites, thrills, or hurts or numbs – as being male can also be painful, convey loss, and being taken out, or transported elsewhere.

Male imagos are also culturally elaborate in the mix of pre-formed narratives that frame the relationship-scene (transference). They are not only charged with pre-conceived male roles and styles in relation to gendered other(s) – such as all that trades and is commoditized as machismo – but also incorporate set fixed relational dynamics within maleness, both touch/contact between men, and proscribed role/play, notably between fathers and sons.

There is clearly a politics to this – both on the level of the formal promotion of set versions of male inter-play (such as fathers teaching sons) which are taken to be essential for the development of the normal family romance; and on the level of social fantasy-enhancement (advertisement) of prescribed male interactive skills to promote this normal family scheme, notably the sale of anything that authorizes (branded) male strength to fix or regulate abnormal/deviant situations. This strength is routinely displaced in adverts to inflating the size and resilience of muscles that take over and win disputes/sports between men.

The repetitive thrust of these normative politics actively encrusts the improvised elaboration of male imagos. It pre-scripts or rings off recommended (primal) scenes/spots to be male, and fictionally attempts to short-circuit the impact of the other(ness) in the transference underlying these scenes. This basic fictional work takes place culturally on all levels where men reflect upon themselves (the news), entertain themselves (the media), or sell things to each other (the market). To take up work in these fields involves buying in to a certain male rhetoric – assuming a male speaker position, speaking from male authority, employing a defined skills-set (strength), and using the correct language/proscribed action (male cool) to address whatever emerges as an issue. This everyday male rhetoric is therefore both normative – it generates what should be said and who is in the right position to say it – and authoritative – it empowers (self-authorizes) certain male-speaker-forms and male topics of speech/action/communication (e.g., Men Behaving Badly). Of course, as the rhetoric visibly fails to capture the other(ness) in being male – and the subsequent on-going contusion generated in the transference begins to obtrude – those rhetorically/authoritatively self-empowered as male attempt artificially to restore the norm(ative). They try rhetorically to inflate the authority invested in their formal male-speaker position, but the resistance of the other(ness) (the unconscious process in transference) of being male empties out the desired transparency of the communication, and renders their authority increasingly shallow and opaque (authoritarian) (See Adorno et al, 1950). So the more this rhetoric attempts to restore the normal, the more it encrusts its imagos and degenerates into cliché; and the more too its set authoritative personalities (above all fathers) become authoritarian (truth managers).

Perhaps the most powerful cliché surrounding being male links male(ness) to violence. Ultimately being male links to restoring authority through imposing physical strength. This cliché has various culturally elaborated supports, ranging from biological determinism – where testosterone is supposed to prompt male violence – to some popular psychological typology – where being male is supposed to connote cold, dominant, un-emotional and un-responsive behaviour. It is no surprise then that the general cultural support for this cliché – notably the form of its fictional amplification – runs counter to the marked decline in its contemporary technical support. Technically, in terms of violence, modern weapons have effectively removed the significance of disproportionate (male) strength. So cliché compensation to restore the male authority to violence re-locates to an obvious culturally flagged site where boys are invited to engage with all the pre-conceived fictional dimensions of (paternal) power. In particular, the cartoon and computer-graphic virtual world offers an ideal (fantasy-amplified) virtual site to supplement the increasingly vacuous and gratuitous significance of male violence. Cartoon and computer-console-game characters prodigiously feature in primal scenes between men, and endlessly amplify their male capacity to obliterate the other(ness) without come-back (contusion). These characters are more male in their violence than (normal) male (*He-Man*); they have tireless weapons and kill indiscriminately (*Terminator*); and they are morphed round wild animals, they can fly, and (what a surprise) they tend to have dutiful 'sons' who are next in line for super male(ness) (*Batman/Spiderman/Superman*). Their cartoon/virtual narrative form foregrounds both their fantasy and fictional status; and enables the narrative fluidity of their violence – that is, to survive obliteration/redundancy/insignificance, and re-morph as violent as male as may be. To survive and persist in their virtual world, such male characters have artificially to fill in (theorize or provide narrative connections) for all that is missing/lacking/not known in being male in the on-going scene – namely the fissures punctured by the other(ness) that closes down the game (the transference). Hence the correlative production of narrative supplements – notably the books of cheats that proliferate around console games to short-cut (through knowledge) unforeseen narrative blockages, and to avoid wipe-out (or the destructive feed-back of violence/contusive male(ness)). (Adams draws similar conclusions regarding the aggressive properties of computer games and their detrimental effects on the identity of boys in her 'The Myth of Latency: Constructing Boyhood, Labour and Desire', Chapter 3 in this book).

Such violent male clichés therefore invariably generate their own Chernobyl effect. They pour in masses of narrative virtual concrete to stem the transference feed-back generated by the inflation of encrusted male imagos (around the gratuitous authority of violent acts). They may well work on the level of giving pleasure to millions of (male) gamers, but the problem (of other(ness) in transference) displaces to the after-effects (in normative reality). Such virtual male imagos encapsulating violent authority potentially either heighten the expectation of being violent as being male and therefore inevitably accentuate the disappointment/confusion/sense of lack of male(ness) of not being violent (in reality); or conversely, these virtual male imagos close down the affective link to male(ness) altogether and install either alienation (affective separation from being male – because this male(ness) is intentionally non-real) or aphanisis (lack of desire in connection to this fantasy construction of male – because violence may be repulsive).

It is not the place here to go further into the politics of this – which hopefully will continue not to work on the level of installing, restoring, or reinforcing the significance and authority of macho outpourings in all interpersonal exchange! Suffice it to say that if the games themselves do not suspend belief – and it is the good liberal belief that boys know they are not really killing people – belief in being (violent) male itself will be suspended in the transference. All from the other that is raw, sensorial, and unprocessed (unconscious) in the male imago will inevitably impact on any sense of being male. The subsequent contusions will likely subvert if not close down any recognition as male (cognitive transparency) from the other, so suspend all intercourse. As with all violent exchange, the life-blood is likely to flow and the contusions will be dramatic!

Re-processing male imagos in the primal scene

The contusion issuing from male imagos in the ambient re-working of the primal scene, is generated by the subversion of set story-lines that pre-construct the male position/role, by more primary unconscious (unprocessed) sensorial-affect-elements trapped within the image-component of the imago, which subsequently resonate with male(ness). The dramatic effect – and extent – of this contusion derives from the hugely elaborate cultural pre-script that prompts the primal scene – notably all the epic dimensions that bifurcate the couple-in-intercourse into male and female, mother and father, and penis-in-vagina. But, as we have seen, the primary sensorial-affect-elements are neither necessarily gender-bifurcated – there is equally importantly a male-to-male potential space in the primal scene; nor do these primary sensorial-affect-elements necessarily constellate around a generative parental couple – they can equally involve the rival or identification-fused father/son duo; nor are these primary elements necessarily body-sourced in the penis, vagina, or combined penis/vagina – bodies do not simply or naturally inter-lock, they also variously and imperfectly (in a non-aligned way) press together.

In this alternative male-to-male context, a crucial primary dynamic encapsulated in the primal scene elaborates around wrestling. Wrestling both amalgamates a complex mix of elaborate and distinct drives – such as aggression, playfulness, eroticism and competitiveness (sport); and it engages a mix of whole and part bodies in coordinated movement (intercourse) – but vitally it does not directly (con)figure or feature the penis. Wrestling also installs and promotes a potential primary sensorial-affect space in the primal scene – a touch space generated around the ongoing interpersonal dynamics of grip and squeeze, with fraught potential contusions mixing pleasure and pain. It is significantly weapon-less – though clearly macho politics will attempt to exploit this touch space by supplementing it (or symbolically inflating its violent potential) with weapons. This potential male touch-space of wrestling can readily and variously compact and subvert classic gender-bifurcated primal scene narratives – not least to body-slam – or suddenly de-eroticize and castrate (de-phallicize) the central (parental) embrace – substituting pres-sure of one (part)body on another, with all the profuse and complex affects that may induce, as opposed to the fantasised release associated with synchronized phallic penetration and vaginal absorption (parental intercourse). Furthermore, wrestling adds a rich further layer to the nar-rative elaboration of the primal scene – above all, the cultural history of chivalry, in which men face men (inter-male honour) to defend the name/honour of their lord/father/family/clan. Traditionally too, these inter-male wrestling contests were/are performed before an exclusively male audience.

Beowulf – the Anglo-Saxon/Scandinavian epic – provides a classic, culturally-rich site to explore the male-to-male dynamics of wrestling, and its complex role in constructing a male-effect independent of a primary (copulating) parental couple in the primal scene. Beowulf – the hero – is renown for wrestling with the elements, even though he once lost a swimming contest with Breca (because he was waylaid by 'sea brutes wild'): 'You waded in', Unferth tells him, 'embracing water, taking its measure, mastering currents, riding on the swell. The ocean swayed, winter went wild in the waves, but you vied for seven nights; and then he outswam you, came ashore the stronger contender' (p. 35). Beowulf chooses to appeal to these raw wrestling skills against the dreaded enemy Grendel, precisely because Grendel is a wild force of nature (a monster): 'He (Grendel) has no idea of the arts of war, of shield or sword-play, although he does possess a wild strength. No weapons, therefore, for either this night; unarmed he shall face me if he dares' (p. 47). And, of course, Grendel succumbs to Beowulf 'in a handgrip harder than anything he had ever encountered in any man on the face of the earth' (p. 51).

Beowulf's subsequent wrestling bout complicates the story. On the one hand, it is simply provoked by a family duty to revenge – in this case, Grendel's mother's parental duty to avenge her son. It is important here that her gender does not preclude her occupying a male place in the wrestling exchange. The text highlights this: 'Her onslaught was less only by as much as an amazon warrior's strength is less than an armed man's when the hefted sword, its hammered edge and gleaming blade slathered in blood, razes the sturdy boar-ridge off a helmet' (p. 89). The complication relates to her history – the events in her (family) life that do not concord with the (male) chivalric position: 'Grendel's mother, monstrous hell-bride, brooded on her wrongs. She had been forced down into fearful waters, the cold depths, after Cain had killed his father's son, felled his own brother with a sword' (p. 87).

So the wrestling match adds significant supplements: the imagos of the cold depths and the sword – images that encapsulate unprocessed affects issuing from previous re-workings of wrestling within primal scenes. In transference resonance to this, Beowulf musters his own specific symbolic supplement (imago) – his chain-mail shirt (*byrnie*), a family heir-loom. The primal scene re-working that ensues entwines primal wrestling (grip) with symbolic pre-scripting (supplements) – notably in the inter-course between the sword and *byrnie* imagos, in which his heirloom sword (*Hrunting*) visibly fails, and eventually melts: 'So she (Grendel's mother) lunged and clutched and managed to catch him (Beowulf) in her brutal grip; but his body, for all that, remained unscathed: the mesh of the chain-mail saved him on the outside. Her savage talons failed to rip the web of his war-shirt. Then once she touched bottom, that wolfish swimmer carried the ring-mailed prince to her court so that for all his courage he could never use the weapons he carried; and a bewildering horde came at him from the depths, droves of sea-beasts who attacked with tusks and tore at his chain-mail in a ghastly onslaught' (p. 103). As his chain-mail held out, it remained for him to slam dunk the scene/story by wounding her mortally with an heirloom sword from her own armoury.

In a Hollywood re-work of this epic (pace Jean-Luc Godard's views on US cinema's editing out, montage and history), Robert Zemeckis (2007) significantly edits out the wrestling dynamic of this second bout – so closes the male position for Grendel's mother. Rather than wrestle, she seduces him – armed by her very powerful alternative imago-weapons, her fulsome breasts (this is, of course, reinforced by the viewers' inevitable association of Grendel's mother with *Lara Croft* through the actress Angelina Jolie). Moreover, rather than lose, become wounded, and die, she falls pregnant and provides Beowulf with an heir. Ironically, to stay a-grip of the heroic script, Beowulf has to keep the true version secret, and pretend he has really killed her. So he doubly force-bifurcates the production of male effects: he re-sets the male in the generative parental couple process (intercourse produces the heir) as opposed to the grapple of the inter-male; and he splits off a supplementary level of psychological elaboration of being male around the lie – which is contusively elaborated in the f(r)iction caused by substituting the on-going piercing sword and resistant *byrnie* (chain-mail shirt) intercourse, with the 'normal' pre-script imposed unilaterally by the generative paternal penis imago. But that's Hollywood!

A case of male contusion

John, a 42 year-old gay fashion designer, comes into analysis complaining he has completely lost the plot. He is totally unclear how he lost the plot, or why he lost it when he did. He then describes a topsy-turvy sequence of events in which he suddenly loses power in relationship to his long-term partner, Shane, and starts to feel colourless and invisible – both terms are anathema to a fashion designer at the height of his visibility. Above all, he complains of losing all sense of being male – something he was proud and sure of before, like some publicly acclaimed fashion design.

The events he describes actually turn around Shane visibly losing the plot. First of all, Shane shaved off his beard, which he had carefully trimmed since he was an adolescent. Then Shane took to withdrawing frequently to his room – or once to the corner of some bar – to scribble reams of improvised verse – which John discovered surreptitiously to describe in elaborate detail (and Shane was just a simple bloke) gratuitous sexual encounters with strangers. When questioned about these encounters, Shane was consummately unperturbed. He smiled and authoritatively confessed it was great fun, particularly following on from 7 years of monogamy with John. After the confession, Shane started to stay out all night, and John started to stay home regularly just waiting. One evening in a bar, a stranger came up to John to warn him about Shane. He said he had had sex with Shane several times, and each time Shane had luxuriated in poking fun of John, particularly his lovemaking. Two days later, Shane disappeared, presumably for good. He left no written explanation. He left all his clothes with John. John found both the police and friends remarkably unperturbed, as if they knew something he did not know. John was left cut off entirely from the male bond (knowledge), which was once spontaneous, or at least well understood.

Sifting through the debris, John stuck with the thought/scene of Shane first shaving off his beard. John was very struck by Shane's beard, particularly by the profuse tuft on his chin, and the clean-shaven lines that bordered it. He recalled the first blow job that Shane had given him, and the extreme excitement of seeing this tuft engulf his penis. Much to his horror, after Shane shaved off his beard, John lost all desire, his erection, and his sense of being male. Why (he asked)?

Primal scene elements emerged in free associative exploration of this sudden stalling in John's relation to Shane. The stalling evoked two powerful transference effects: the sense of fatally wounded maleness, and the loss of sexual power and desire which was somehow vitally attached to it. For John, the central image that seemed to underlie both his attraction to Shane, and his own visceral connection to being male, was the beard. Within the beard image, there lay a particular resonance around the tuft. When he reflected on the process that may underlie his free associative construction of the scene – what continuously gripped his attention and drove on his intricate elaborations – he was struck in particular by the act of shaving. The shaving process though seemed permanently to be stuck at one stage removed – in the other person (Shane). John's principal question remained "what drove Shane to shave (his beard)?" The vital issue of why this shaving impacted so powerfully on John himself seemed curiously less evocative and urgent.

The imago that emerged in John's primal scene re-workings in analysis encapsulated and amalgamated specific beard/tuft/shaving resonances. In particular, in free association, John recalled the beard his father had worn when John was about seven. John actually remembered it as a 'closely cropped' beard, but was always 'surprised' by photos from that time that showed the beard to be 'wild and profuse'. John speculated that this could be because he had always experienced his father to be psychologically 'closely cropped'. The man was an eminent brain surgeon, who was rarely at home, and always remained stiff, formal and remote. People would stop teenager John in the street to tell him what an amazing man his father was, what a pillar of society he was, and how warm and generous he was with patients. John had no idea at all who this man was, and not a clue either how this male-double might co-habit the cold crusty patriarch he thought he knew. This clash of different males co-habiting in his father reached a major crescendo when John tried to come out (as a homosexual) to him. The cold immaculately-shaven figure who told John he was disappointed by his passionate revelation, was never someone John could imagine sporting a wild and profuse beard. If his father ever wore a beard – despite the photographic evidence – he would have taken a crop to it and savagely trimmed it back.

Exploring further the resonances of the tuft shaved out from the wild beard, John fell upon another poignant scene that seemed inlaid or stuck in an image from his early childhood. He was on holiday in Italy with his parents, and awoke one hot afternoon to observe them embracing in the adjoining bed. Although he was aware that they were both naked, he was both confused and curious about how their bodies were aligned. A thick tuft of bright red hair stood out between their entwined bodies, and he was totally unclear whether it belonged to his father – whether it was his beard or some other body hair – or whether it belonged to his mother (he even thought she might too have suddenly sprouted a beard) – or whether in some way they shared it, and it moved/lived independently of both of them. In his repeated later re-visits to this scene, John was struck by two particularly resonant features. First, that the tuft was red, and both his parents had dark black hair – though he had always loved the colour red, and his fashion design work prominently featured it. Of course, Shane's red hair/trimmed beard had instantly struck/grabbed him. Secondly, on reflection, John was intrigued that his father's penis did not figure in the scene at all. He speculated in hindsight that the scene may well have actually involved cunnilingus between his father and mother, but he did not experience it as clear and as closed as that. The enigmatic power and excitement lay rather in the tuft itself that mysteriously attached itself to his father's trimmed beard. It was the trimmed beard – and not the (absent) penis – that evoked being male for him.

Conclusion: Constructing a new male – theatre or factory?

To recap: male(ness) can be seen to constitute a charged effect in a fictional elaboration (primal scene) that is continuously woven and re-vamped around primary desire(s) with other(s). This male effect is generated in turn by imagos that encapsulate and amalgamate in redolent images the various bits of ambient narrative attached by the person to the (cultural) position of male. Imagos incorporate as well the raw unprocessed unconscious material (transference), anchored in progressive (primal) scenes that bond the person through affect to significant other(s). In intercourse with other(s), imagos variously press, rub, resonate, and clash with other material within the transference. The ensuing contusion freely mixes a wide range of affects: in this way, (being) male can feel equally painful as pleasurable and joyful.

I am sitting on a London bus at evening rush-hour watching passengers climb on board, find their bearings, and look for a place to stand or sit. There is a simple theatre to it, as people climb on individually to face a seated audience. Suddenly caught in the gaze of this motley bunch of strangers, people become aware that they stand out in their own particular way: how they look, dress, speak or move. There are set parts to play in getting to your determined space: whether and how to say 'excuse me' or 'sorry' as you pass people, or ask them to move; whether and how to make eye or physical contact; whether to smile, or make a facial expression, or to speak at all (even rhetorically to oneself).

In this theatrical bustle, I am struck by the broad pastiche of male effects. There are classic studied macho effects: builders kitted in dirty tight jeans and tee-shirts, emblazoned in tattoos, who shout crudely to each other, and try to swagger their way past, through and over everyone else; or cool macho would-be athletes, who wear their designer sportswear outfits all day everywhere, and need to splay their muscular legs so wide to take up two seats, and then appear too engrossed in their i-pods to hear repeated calls to move – till some other classic macho style eventually imposes to put them in their place. In contrast, there are the studied chivalric male effects: the young woman in school uniform who jumps to her feet to offer her seat to an elderly gentleman; or the elderly gentleman (surrounded by seated adolescents) who alone offers his seat to a pregnant woman. The resonant accent here is on the gentle – knightly or noble – in gentleman – where it was once considered a male prerogative to open doors or offer seats (even the last ones in lifeboats) to ladies. Finally, there are the studied wrestling male effects: the smart suited business-woman who forcibly shifts her hips to push her neighbour firmly back in place; or the bespectacled bald man with polka-dot tie, who drops his copy of the *Financial Times* to catch a falling neighbour who lost her balance, then turn her round, put her back on her feet, and return to reading – all without uttering a word.

In all cases, the performance elements of these male effects are pre-coded and prescribed. Even the dress(code) – be it suit or tee-shirt (both male in this context but formally un-gendered) – mark out some expected (male) effect for the performer. In this way, there is a vital element of cliché and parody in even the most seemingly naïve and automatic male performances of this kind. Even the most unrepentant macho virtuoso performance knows that the imago that seemingly holds the desired male-effect is vitally flawed – and it cracks open when some (macho) other holds up the mirror to show what it lacks (the fiasco). This cliché/parody/fiasco element of male(ness) installs itself through, and in, the on-going self-theorization surrounding primal scene(s). Theorizing what is going on in – and between – significant other(s) in turn generates its own theoretical (reverberative) encrustation: people come to think they know what expectation underlies a male effect. It is seemingly simple to turn this effect on in/between the other – as simple as turning on a light-bulb. But therein (in such knowledge) lies the fiasco.

It is precisely at this self-theorization level that lies the fundamental problematic of male(ness): namely, can the production of all the negative clichés of male(ness) – all the brute violence, insensitivity, and destructiveness – actively be changed? It has been argued here that there must be an inevitable unconscious subversion of such clichés in transference with other(s), and that the singular elaborative contusions generated around imagos will continuously drive revisions of male(ness) based on shifting affect. But the question remains of how this can and will impact on the everyday political manipulation of male(ness) discussed earlier – in particular the cartoon promotion of an authoritarian version of masculinity that elsewhere (in transference/intercourse) visibly fails?

As we have seen, Freud aimed to normalize this unconscious subversion by locking it exclusively in to family dynamics: the primal scene – and the potential identification of/with being male (and female/feminine) – revolved entirely around the father's intercourse with the mother. Revisions of this Oedipal scheme questioned its phallic privilege but kept its family frame. The generative couple potentially balanced (assumed) male excess. Even psychologically, the new man should emerge from acknowledging and giving rightful place to the maternal in the inner generative couple – balancing animus with anima. To their huge credit, Gilles Deleuze and Felix Guattari (1968) threw down the gauntlet (to follow family chivalry) – or threw a spanner in the works (to follow their industrial analogy) – of/to family recuperation of (so-called) male violence. By suggesting that the factory rather than the (family) theatre was a more apt place to work with the production of masculinity, they drew attention both to the exploitative dynamics of the family, and its role in masking basic (violent/power) contradictions in the capitalist system as a whole. Even more important, they exposed the politics of attempting to recuperate in virtual reality what is lacking (in male effect/affect) in reality – in short (what underlies) the intimate link between capitalism and schizophrenia.

From all that has been argued here, it would be easy to conclude that male(ness) will imminently collapse under loss of affect – provoked by the substitution of virtual for real (relational) gratification. This view fails to take account of the wild singular and transformative powers of the unconscious, and how fundamental shifts that occur in transference re-align people with their raw creative energies. Being male in this increasingly managed everyday world will undoubtedly become ever more complex, but direct grappling with complexities was ever an epic and transformative element of male(ness). People just need to find within their own lives how and when to lay down their weapons (above all knowledge).

3
The Myth of Latency and the Construction of Boyhood

Tessa Adams

What interests me in this chapter are certain unresolved questions surrounding boyhood from a psychoanalytic perspective, in particular that period of sexual moratorium referred to by Freud as latency. The onset of latency is seen to occur when the infant boy at the age of four to five years is understood to unconsciously relinquish desire for the mother (the source of original Oedipal conflict) through the prospect of securing a positive identification with the father and with the male group. That is to say, latency is that period in which male privilege is forged out of the infant boy's necessity to repudiate maternal relationship. Fundamental to this concept of a mandatory infant sexual moratorium is the belief that, for the junior years, boyhood remains dominated by specific repressive strategies which displace primary object love – instinctual infant desire – in the service of socialization. In other words, this is a concept which promotes a temporary desire-less state (ending at the onset of puberty) as the striking characteristic of boyhood years, that is, a temporary cessation of sexual interest is maintained by compensatory identifications and sublimations. It is argued that this breach (that questions the young male's experience of his boyhood body) heralds the first awareness of sexual inhibition which remains a legacy of conflict throughout life. As Laplanche and Pontalis (1983) point out, latency is 'a pause in sexuality (and) a desexualisation of the emotions (which brings with it) the emergence of such feelings as shame and disgust along with aesthetic aspirations' (p. 234).

The psychoanalytic and social construction of the 'Latent' Boy

The Freudian notion of 'latency' offers an analysis of libidinal transformation that indicates that the potent desires of infancy give way to social

38

imperative, leading to repression, on the one hand, and sublimation, on the other. Put simply, Freud claims that the solution for the little boy (in the throes of Oedipal conflict) is for the spontaneous innocence of desiring infancy to be eclipsed by the imperative for male identification. Thus, male identification is conceived as heralding a gap in sensuality in which potential shaming by the male group results in a necessary turning away from all that the mother represents. That is to say, all the freedoms of infant bodily expression become overwhelmed by social responsibility of which the male group, signified by the father, remains sovereign. It is clear that this image of the desire-less boy with attendant compensatory male identifications has influenced the Western construct of boyhood. But the question that arises here is: could it be that to frame a period of psycho-sexual development as 'latent' has been socially convenient, especially, since the principle of latency offers a justification for the tender emotions of infancy, in the case of the boy, to remain irrevocably split from manhood? In other words, we can consider whether, or not, the social and psychoanalytic construction of the latent boy, in his apparent release from the conflict of desire, serves the collective in terms of male bargaining for profit and power.

Otherwise, a question can be raised from the opposite standpoint: does this principle of boyhood desexualization, in which Freud proposes male identification rupturing sensual attachment to mother, reflect the actual social positioning that the young Western male, historically, has been expected to take? This is to suggest that Freud, in naming the junior male as subject to a moratorium of desire, by which affection and tenderness towards the mother are supplanted by paternal identifications, could simply be illuminating the emotional status that has been socially permitted to boyhood.

If the economic benefits of boyhood apprenticeships of the past are considered, it is not difficult to recognize what might be gained from ensuring that the affections of erotic boyhood be repressed for the purposes of a materialistic male bonding. There is no doubt that boyhood apprenticeship, in providing a contract for the 'boy-becoming-man', would greatly benefit from harnessing the passions of the junior boy's developmental transition in which paternal identification invariably would promise a legacy of submissive service. In the history of boyhood labour it is clear that it would have been problematic for desire to play its part in an environment in which working fathers would witness young boys struggling with the tiredness of adult tasks. Much better that boys be seen to be passionless; in lacking desire they neither would be subject to fear, nor would they be in the need of love and compassion.

When certain rituals that initiate boys into manhood are investigated, the determination that young boys should survive without emotional demand is certainly borne out. Public schools in Britain, for example, are renowned for institutionalizing challenges designed to 'toughen boys up'. There are also the examples of apprenticeship initiations which, in past centuries, would include a level of permitted abuse as the agency of transition from boyhood to manhood. Such practices as the ritual of 'stripping, tarring and feathering', for example, were meted out to ten and twelve year old boys in Britain the early part of last century. This purposeful humiliating act of covering the young apprentice's naked body with warm tar and chicken feathers was a ritual designed to warn the newcomer of the fact that joining the male group required the control of any emotional expression. It is difficult to imagine mothers witnessing such a violation to the bodies of their young, yet many would have been drawn to collude in the support of such rituals as the necessary condition for their son's acceptance by the male group. Since poverty was to be avoided at all cost and apprenticeship secured both training and employment in the mine, factory and steel foundry, who would dare to protest at even the harshest of rites of passage?

At the time that Freud was formulating his conception of latency, within the deprived rural environments of Germany young boys would have been readily put to use. Even the youngest could feed chickens, milk cows and clean out stables. Arguably, the contemporary climate of today's boyhood is vastly different in which self-expression is fostered and child labour is illegal. Does this suggest that boyhood emotions have now a more considered place, and if so, would this indicate that the latent boy is simply a figment of Freud's boyhood past? Yet, if we think of the valid passions by which contemporary boyhood is characterized, this does not seem to be the case. For it is significant that images of contemporary boyhood indicate that love and sensual desire are hardly seen to play their part in the junior years. Rather, the junior/latent boy is characterized predominantly by one emotion, namely, the impulse for aggression in its various legitimized forms. Typically, at school boys are bullied if they appear not to 'stand up for themselves'. Furthermore, a culture of aggression, rather than sensitivity, is instituted by boy's play: for example, boyhood sports are noted for their training of aggressivity; computer games such as 'game-boy' emphasize skill in the player's attacks on fictional enemies, and so on. I would argue that the co-ordinates of male humiliation are still operating to sculpt boyhood, rendering the boy's tender relationship with the mother in question (for a thorough analysis of the effects of computer games on the intensification of the aggressivity of boys, see Stanton's 'Wrestling with Male(ness): Deconstructing the Virtual Macho World in Psychoanalysis and Culture', Chapter 2 in this book).

Before broadening this discussion further, it will be useful to look at the way in which the concept of latency was originally outlined. First, it is important to emphasize that Freud's view of a desire-less post-Oedipal boyhood has apparently taken root. That is to say, historically, Freud's Oedipal analysis of the infant boy has been appropriated (within the psychoanalytic profession and across a range of cultural theory) without significant masculinist critique. This is a position of acceptance which contrasts the wealth of feminist debate that has focused on Freud's psycho-sexual analysis of the infant girl in which Oedipal theory has been significantly criticized. But what kind of boy is it that Freud has portrayed?

In the first instance, Freud's theory of the infantile sexual neurosis is essentially determined by masculine parameters. For although Freud sees the infantile sexual neurosis as equally relevant to the infant girl, he acknowledges a certain lack of theoretical resolution in respect of the female subject (see Freud, 1905). Thus, to a certain extent the Oedipal conflict of the infant boy has become paradigmatic. What this means is that at the centre of the Oedipal drama we find a boy-child, in the first flush of genital awareness, directing primary erotic longing towards that vital maternal body that brought him into being. Freud emphasizes that the strength of this Oedipal fixation is such that the inquisitive infant, at about three years old, embarks on his first conquest, the attempt to possess the mother. Yet, this ambition brings with it a deterrent that will haunt him throughout life, namely, the fear of castration. Thus desire and repudiation synchronize to generate the Oedipal resolution. Freud's rationale for this conflict rests on the specificity of female genitalia that are seen to lack the determinant of which provoke the infant boy's forfeiting of Oedipal longing and thereby essential relationship with mother.

In other words, Freud bases this transformation of libidinal desire on the premise that the infant boy, in the advent of genital preoccupation, perceives the mother's absence of penis as the signification of castration and, in rivalry with the father, casts the father as potential aggressor/ castrator. What this means is that the infant boy shuns maternal solicitude in fear of losing penile security and, through the process of identification, turns towards the male provider to protect rather than castigate (see Freud, 1905). Clearly, framing the Oedipal drama as pivotal in terms of the infant's psycho-sexual development is a powerful analysis. For here we have a boy-infant identified as male competitor relinquishing the nurturing maternal body in fear of the adult male aggressor, ironically his own father. Humiliated, in protection of his prized body part, the boy-child is seen to affect a compromise. In other words, both in fear and in awe, turning away from the feminine, a compensatory strategy is conceived, since the Oedipal crisis is seen to be resolved through the process of identification with masculine potency, exemplified by the father who, in fantasy, could have vanquished him. Thus the scene is set for a narrative of male bonding, out of which desire and compassion are subdued and maternal attachment subordinated.

What this means is that amidst this libidinal scenario, on which the cornerstone of psychoanalysis rests, an image of challenged boyhood summons us. An image of male infant omnipotence journeying towards the possession of his own mother only to be deterred by a vision of the superior male competitor, his own father, potentially rendering him impotent; a state that he believes his mother has endured before him. In the face of such terror, the recourse for the boy child (in his identification with paternal supremacy) is to retreat into a libidinal never-never-land, namely latency, from which position the social split between boyhood and manhood is instigated. For within this anticipated moratorium, emotional expression for the boy is both desexualized and identified as potentially abhorrent. Thus the myth of effortless boyhood is furnished, and if challenged by circumstances that emphasize boyhood sensuality as robust and possibly dangerous, language is defeated. We only have to be reminded of the confusion surrounding those cases in which boyhood eroticization is publicly identified to realize the weight of the social construction of latency. Boys who break the code of desire-less latency are invariably profiled as 'monsters' by the press to denote the exception of their sexualized expression. In such circumstances it is as if the individual transgressor has permanently sullied the prospect of innocent boyhood.

We can now see how Freud constructs this dominant fiction of desire-less boyhood, in which the instinctual passions of infancy, through fear of castration, are unconsciously held in check during the junior years. It is at puberty that the period of latency is seen to transform into the features of competitive manhood, at which time the residual infant memories of desire for the mother are seen to be reactivated only to be relinquished once again in the wake of the social imperative of the incest taboo. Thus, according to Freud, manhood is emotionally expensive, since the boy child's maturing journey is apparently one of significant loss. In the first place, innocent babyhood abruptly ends with the infant's discovery of his own genital. A discovery, not of joy, but of unparalleled fear, in the face of his mother's absence of a penis and his father's potency, precipitating the infant into a realm of conflict, located as the 'infantile sexual neurosis' (Freud, 1905). In the second place, this conflict of desire is mitigated, but through a process of adaptation in which identification plays the fullest part; and desire, emotionality and maternal need from this point on remain significantly repressed. It is interesting to note that Nancy Chodorow (1978), in her book *The Reproduction of Mothering*, touches upon these issues by identifying how the infant boy's turning away from the mother offers a level of autonomy, fuelled by the capacity to fully identify with the parent of the same sex that is denied to the female subject. Her concern is that women suffer from a distorted identification with mothering, rather than 'mother' stating 'for the girl, identification is likely to be – at best – with the mother's maternality rather than with her as an active sexual being' (Chodorow, 1994, p. 60). But while Chodorow sees the boy's development as less repressed than that of the girl, she proposes that the societal privileging of masculinity, in which male superiority is applauded, engender boyhood identifications that leave the male subject caught up in a web of the denial of maternal attachment.

Representing/reproducing the 'Latent' boy in Western art

Now to return to the central question of this chapter, namely, why is it that latency remains such an enduring interpretation of the status of boyhood desire, both in terms of its social purpose and in terms of psychoanalytic justification? Is the image of the latent boy the one that we simply wish to maintain or is it a descriptor of the status of boyhood that is culturally the most prevalent? In order to address this question historically it is useful to analyse the images of boyhood that have dominated the Western economy. That is to say, it is relevant to consider how boyhood is literally depicted through certain imagery that is readily available, and in particular those images of boyhood perpetuated through the legacy of classical painting. What I am suggesting here is that we have undoubtedly ingested images of boyhood that have been aestheticized and deified, but the question that is raised here is, what kind of boyhood has been made manifest in the inspiring images of classical art that have haunted and seduced the viewer over centuries? In other words, how has the boy-subject been historically configured within Western society through the dominance of Western art?

In analysing the iconography of boyhood within Renaissance and post-Renaissance painting, it is evident that certain features of boyhood not only predominate but are significantly subscribed to today. That is to say, there is no doubt that the infant boy has been canalized as a decorative feature in both devotional and allegorical narratives. But what is relevant to this discussion on latency is that, while we are familiar with the saturation of infant images of cherubs and putti that adorn much of representational painting of the sixteenth and seventeenth centuries, there remains a contrast with the paucity of the positioning of boyhood as subject. In other words, it is noticeable that within the history of the painted narrative the infant boy has been copiously signified as agency, leaving the junior boy, as subject, virtually annexed. Yet there exists a striking exception, namely, the images of the boyhood of Christ.

Let us consider in more detail the ways in which boyhood serves both classical and religious narratives. First and foremost the plethora of infant adornment (manifest by the cherubs and putti) is accepted as an integral feature of devotional painting. That is to say, we expect to absorb this adornment, concerning ourselves neither with the implications for boyhood nor the fugitive affect on manhood. But, as signifiers (from a psychoanalytic perspective) the way that these cherubs are indulgently painted – cast as both playful and robustly sensual – it is possible to think of that which is lost in boyhood through the advent of latency. Typically, the putto/cherub is male and in the reverie of adornment can be seen to be neither the key aspect of the narrative nor expendable. Does this not suggest that these cherubs (invariably depicted as fleeting in glance and posture) in their sensual delight can be seen to be representing the infant boy's anticipated rupture from the maternal body? Furthermore, in studying the role of the cherubs/putti, we find them consistently profiled as subjects whose purpose is to draw attention to the site of forbidden desire by either directing attention to a devotional moment, for example, within the Nativity of the Christian tradition, or the enhancing of sensual exchange within the classical narrative. It is as if these sensuous infants signify that moment when the adored-imaged-body of infancy is to become the absent-imaged-body of latency. In other words, we can interpret these playful infants as the Oedipal subject on the cusp of latency. That is, standing at once at the site of passion, but preparing to break apart and seek paternal identification in the bid for attachment to the superior 'knowledge' of the male group.

What is significant about this paradoxical infant depiction that is conveyed by the cherub/putto, is that we meet the infant boy in a conflictual position. Exuberant in his labours, for he is essentially called to assist desire, he appears to be fully attentive to the site of pleasure, on the one hand, while, on the other, is hardly permitted the joy of the maternal gaze, since even in the baroque of cherubic excesses we see the gaze of the putto is largely diverted. What I have emphasized here is that it is remarkable that so much painting should exhibit a preoccupation with infant boyhood which frames the child as facilitator nurturing the desiring moment, yet so often turning away from the directness of the libidinal glance. As the infant Cupid so often exemplifies, this is truly a male quest in which this dynamic of transformation plays the fullest part, for example, depictions of Venus typically portray Cupid holding the mirror so that Venus can admire her beauty, yet he coyly ducks his head indicating that he is not permitted the desiring gaze (see Figure 3.1).

In the context of the many angelic cascading bodies, which decorate much devotional painting, it seems appropriate to interpret the infant subject's sensual delight as materially displaced in Oedipal terms. The question to be asked, in the light of this favoured image of infancy (which certainly overshadows other effective boyhood depiction) is whether, or not, these limited male representations have some bearing upon the socially permitted status of boyhood desire? Certainly, as I have

Figure 3.1   Velazquez, *The Rokeby Venus* (c. 1650) National Gallery, London.

intimated, the images of libidinal, cavorting infancy, typically portrayed by cherubs and putti, would satisfy the Freudian premise of an eruption of infantile sexual desire which is to be repressed and sublimated. Certainly too, the sensual reverie that these naked infants represent is one that boyhood (in latency) apparently has the task to subdue. What I am suggesting here is that this dynamic of Oedipal desire, exemplified by the infant boy apprehending sensuality, yet mindful of taboo, can seem to be configured throughout classical and devotional narratives. By way of illustration it is valuable to consider the work of the seventeenth century French classicist, Nicolas Poussin, and in particular his well known painting *Rinaldo and Armida* (Figure 3.2).

In this painting Armida, a heathen, embarks upon a murderous quest when she stumbles across the defenceless Christian warrior, Rinaldo. With sword and shield cast down (in a child like slumber) Rinaldo appears to be oblivious of his fate. Yet, it is a winged putto who is summoned to his rescue. Tugging desperately at Armida's arm, in a flush of sensual anxiety, we see the infant boy struggling to divert Armida's lethal stiletto knife from her grasp. This action is in accord with the purpose of the

Figure 3.2 Poussin, *Rinaldo and Armida* (1629) Dulwich Picture Gallery, London.

painting that is intended to allegorize the Christian ethic, namely, that desire be quenched by reason. It is notable that, since this is a century in which reason would be unequivocally associated with the male, we find that Poussin locates reason within each male posture: the putto in his reasoned tug against danger; Rinaldo (although prostrate) in his gleaming armour of trust. Yet, while we can assume that it is Armida who holds the forbidden desire, it also feasible that Rinaldo, in his spontaneous childlike slumber, can be seen to embrace the very sensuality that is being refuted – so too the putto in his flushed clasping of the maternal body. This leads me to suggest that, at an Oedipal level, both males are similarly identified in their struggle for sublimation: Rinaldo, in what appears to be a submissive sensual posture; the putto in the urgent tactile clasping of the female arm so near the naked breast. In other words, although desire for the conquering 'mother' (Armida) is being challenged, it remains not entirely repressed. This identification is further emphasized in the mirroring of weapons: the sword of the man (Rinaldo) as phallus and the stiletto of the boy (putto) as penis, both of which appear potentially potent yet indicate that each male could be disarmed. In brief we can interpret this painting as a complex representation of boyhood identification which both signifies male desire and its absence in latency. Since in saving reason from castration the infant/putto has the task of exchanging the stiletto/penis/maternal object for the sword/phallus of the man; but a sword of one who sleeps, namely, that male desire to be awakened from the boyhood slumber of latency.

In other words, the complexity of the erotic task with which this putto is concerned can be seen to typify the psychological position that the infant boy is subliminally asked to confront. I would argue that this image represents both boyhood's evident sensuality, on the one hand, and its problematic position, on the other. Interpreting the painting (psychodynamically) the paradox is thus: if the infant/putto were to sanction the death of the male other in phantasy, both his omnipotent potency and his illusion of the phallic mother would be reinforced. Yet if the mother is disarmed of desire the infant-boy is disarmed also, since she forfeits her power over the slumbering warrior. Arguably, this painting provides a representation for both of these possible consequences, for Poussin, in his painterly precision implies that the stiletto is in the command of both the putto and Armida.

I have focused on the function of the putto within Poussin's *Rinaldo and Armida* as a means by which to emphasize the ways in which boyhood desire is constructed within much of Western painting. There are many other paintings that could be presented to illuminate my hypothesis. But in this context such a lengthy procedure could be less valuable than the prospect of outlining a strategy by which to interpret the portrayal of certain features of boyhood within classical and devotional narratives. In this light I will present the following proposition, namely, that there are three main aspects of depiction of the boy-subject which predominate the Western tradition. While these three categories can be readily located, there is also the factor of a certain overlap to be taken into consideration.

First, there are those paintings which conspicuously exploit the image of infancy as libidinally colluding with the site of desire. These are works in which the imaged infant-boy plays a role in engaging the viewer through their flushed sensual playful bodies, as if in foreplay for a consummating act with the body sublime. It is significant that the sensuality of these little male bodies is further exploited by contemporization in the form of part-objects. Adorning Christmas cards and notelets putti and cherubs are wrenched from context so as sensual delight in them to be increased. Since, with the Christ-child split away the sensual pleasure of these playful joyous infants (drawn from works of Titian, Tintoretto, Raphael and other great masters) can offer the viewer gratification without demanding (of the viewer) devotional responsibility. In other words, we can delight in the exuberance of these fragments without paying attention to the purpose of the original painting. Thus, in a notelet or card, the gaze of the infant can be captured split off from grand narrative that it originally served.

Second, there are those images, as with Poussin, in which latency is anticipated. This is the category in which the putti and cherubs are themselves much deployed in small tasks. In some instances it seems that the labours become more onerous as infancy proceeds. It is as if they are kept busy with the world in order to signify the desire-less state to come, namely, the demand of male identification with its eventual apprenticeship to the group. Here we see the more baby-like configurations (flushed with desire) giving way to older infant depiction in which the turning away from the direct gaze is compensated by attention to the desire of the other. This shift, the gradual drawing away from maternal engagement, is seen to culminate in the fully latent image which neither exhibits involvement within the frame of the gaze, nor the blatant physicality of the infant libidinal putto/cherubic expression. This is boyhood cast as assistant with the sole purpose to serve desire. Still naked, the awkwardness of this realm of boyhood can be seen to far outweigh the *jouissance* of the hedonistic putto. Eyes are turned away, limbs labouring in task – not play, this boy-subject is given way to the project of the other anticipating the solemnity of manhood to come. This depiction of emergent latent boyhood is clearly evident in Michelangelo's painting of *The Creation of Man*. Famously known for the focus of Adam's forefinger in juxtaposition with that of his Creator, ironically the attendant male assistants become overlooked. Yet, when we study the way in which the boy-assistants are illustrated it is striking to notice how clumsy and passionless their presence appear, as they carry the weight of this transcendental moment. Furthermore, it is possible that, typically, these busy assistants are not remembered as part of the narrative.

I suggest that the third category of boyhood representation is clearly more fugitive, in keeping with the prospect that it is the latent boy who resists configuration. That is to say, in studying Renaissance and post-Renaissance art it can appear that the boy, in the full moment of boyhood (notwithstanding puberty), is difficult to locate. This is to suggest that potent boyhood is seen to be taboo in keeping with the imperative of latency. Yet, in contrast (as already mentioned) there many images of Christ in childhood years to be found, not simply as baby, but as the knowing and commanding subject. It can be seen that Michelangelo's *Creation* anticipates this third category in which the depiction of boy is more fugitive but where the productive aspect of the latent boy is certainly pronounced. I would argue that the boy-imaged within this genre draws our interest by virtue of displacement. Boyhood, here, exemplifies the bystander: with eyes averted from the site of passion his gaze is elsewhere. His is not the tender fleeting glance at that maternal body afforded the playful infant/cherub, nor does he garland the world with his own sensuality, rather he stands as reliable attendant, holding, waiting and of use. That is to say, I see this image of boy as more the determined apprentice to the project of adult male desire. In other words, the latent boy is seen to witness desire, but not desiring to take part. He may facilitate or procure sensual gratification for the adult male, yet is presented as remaining separate in wait of the inevitability of post-pubertal consummated passion. These are the images that firmly demonstrate boyhood libidinal disengagement and its displacement in terms of male identification. This boy-subject is given passive tasks, holding armour, looking after animals, etc. – he is no longer available for our delight. This is exemplified by the work of Titian, in his portrayal of seven sons in the painting, *Vandramin Family Venerating a Relic of the True Cross* (Figure 3.3.). Here the sons are clearly placed as bystanders,

Figure 3.3 Titian, *The Vendramin Family Venerating a Relic of the True Cross* (1540–5) National Gallery, London.

one holding a dog, another a hat, and gaze not at the site of Passion, but glance vacantly around.

Furthermore, since the presence of boyhood in this category is demoted, it could be argued that the latent boy (as subject without desire) of necessity will fail to be depicted as the desiring object; since, of that which has been repressed, surely the artist cannot speak. This is to suggest that the subject without desire, the unspoken, will become, to a certain extent, the subject unseen. And how prudently the latent boy remains libidinally mute, for without full representation the image of the Christ child can remain the icon of unchallenged boyhood – the object of divine innocence – reinforcing the prospect that without the conflict of desire there is a site for boyhood to remain the enduring object of passion transcended.

There are of course exceptions to this tendency to which I am referring. One such exception is exemplified by the work of Bronzino, and in particular his *Allegory of Venus and Cupid* (Figure 3.4). Here Cupid is portrayed as sensually seductive: audaciously kissing Venus on the mouth, he holds her breast and gazes into her eyes. Yet there is a level

Figure 3.4   Bronzino, *An Allegory with Venus and Cupid* (c. 1550) National Gallery, London.

of alarm set up within this painting, it as if the pubertal boy is breaking a taboo. For, on the one hand, Venus appears to be receiving Cupid's kisses, while on the other, taking an arrow from his quiver, she is about to pierce his wing.

Conclusion

To summarize, I am arguing that, in studying the actions and glances of the plethora of infant attendants adorning certain devotional/allegorical narratives of sixteenth and seventeenth centuries, we can trace a continuum of pre-pubertal boyhood representation that seems to parallel Freud's principle of infantile sexual neurosis which finds its resolution through male identification. This is to suggest that, just as Freud emphasizes the infant boy's struggle in his developing awareness of the risk in meeting the maternal gaze (which is to be eventually refuted), so too, through painting, this libidinal conflict appears manifest. Thus, I would claim that the cherub/putto, far from appearing 60 simply playfully erotic provides a question to be asked, namely, what is the purpose of these categories of prejudicial boy-subject configurations? I suggest that our imaged saturation of such boy-infant sensuality, culminating in the absent or muted image of the older boyhood years assures that the Freudian principle of boyhood psycho-sexual repression remains configured. And if within this configuration latency, as a moratorium, is seen to justify that boyhood desire be deflected from its gaze through a multitude of servile tasks, surely other references to boyhood passions are in need of representation. Certainly recently there are indications that some contemporary male artists are taking up this concern. Furthermore, there is a prospect that the boy-split-subject's extensive cherubic greeting card presence provides us with the Christ Child as the whole object of maturing boyhood – yet with a desire both innocent and sublime. But, ironically even this transcendent boy-subject is anticipating a virtual 'tarring and feathering' (the Crucifixion) in 'the Name [of identification with] the Father' and withdrawal from mother.

Clearly, as we have seen, there is no reserve in subscribing to the libidinal celebration of the boy infant in the narratives of classical painting in the form of cherub and putto, while the latent boy remains imagistically annexed, and at best portrayed performing servile tasks. If it can be argued that latency as a concept serves the inscription of the desire-less boy-subject and thereby contains that which cannot be spoken or configured, since desiring boyhood appears to fail to be socially incorporated, the question to be raised is what is the driving force of this subterfuge? This is to ask why is it that boyhood is denied its potent image and thereby the prospect of full expression. Furthermore, if latency is simply socially constructed as the libidinal wilderness where the genuine passions of boyhood would be at risk, what is the impact of this moratorium upon manhood passions and sensibilities? This raises issues as to our understanding of masculinity in terms of psychoanalytic assumptions in respect of adult male libidinal desire. For if latency is seen to be a concept socially devised to dismiss the prospect of desiring boyhood, the view that the post-pubertal male is bound to be troubled in terms of 'shame and disgust' (as stated by Laplanche and Pontalis, 1983) by the loss of the ideal state of effortless boyhood passion, could be deconstructed.

4
Narcissism, Mourning and the 'Masculine' Drive

Anastasios Gaitanidis

In this chapter, I will critically engage with Donovan Miyasaki's and Tammy Clewell's attempts to deconstruct Freud's conceptualization of the nature of the drive as 'masculine' and its relation to narcissism and the process of mourning. I have chosen to examine the claims of these two theorists because they adopt (and represent) a current, 'postmodern' approach to Freud's work that I regard as deeply problematic. More specifically, these two theorists argue that, first, Freud's description of the drive as 'masculine' renders the establishment of intersubjective relations impossible and, second, the importance that Freud assigns to the 'masculinistic', narcissistic constitution of the subject gives rise to a theory of mourning which focuses exclusively on the restoration of the mourner's narcissism and not on his/her relation to the lost object. I believe that, despite the provision of useful alternative interpretations of Freud's theory of the drive, narcissism and the process of mourning, the problems these theorists identify – and attempt to solve – in Freud's work are ultimately products of their own *mis*reading of Freud's initial intentions.

Miyasaki's critique of Freud's notion of the 'Masculine' drive

Let us begin with Freud's conceptualization of the nature of the drive. In his *Three Essays on the Theory of Sexuality* (1905) Freud claims that, regardless of an individual's gender or object-choice, the drive (*Trieb*) is intrinsically 'masculine' – at least in the general sense of 'active' as opposed to 'passive' (Freud, 1905, p. 219, note 1). This is trivially true in the sense that the drive actively desires or seeks satisfaction. However,

53

in his paper 'The Evasion of Gender in Freudian Fetishism' Donovan Miyasaki (2003) argues that Freud's description of the drive as 'masculine' applies in a much more specific sense.

Thus, Miyasaki starts his argument by stating that, according to Freud, 'unpleasurable feelings are connected with an increase and pleasurable feelings with a decrease of stimulus' (1915, in Miyasaki, 2003, p. 289). Because sexual tension involves displeasure, the 'aim' of the instinct is 'in every instance satisfaction, which can only be obtained by removing the state of stimulation at the source of instinct' (ibid.). The sexual 'object', on the other hand, is 'the thing in regard to which or through which the instinct is able to achieve its aim' (ibid.). 'Put simply,' Miyasaki states, 'object and aim are the means and end of the sexual instinct. The object is valuable precisely because it is a means to the end of pleasure' (ibid.).

According to Miyasaki, therefore, the active and passive roles of drive and object are embedded in the very nature of pleasure as described by Freud. 'Because the sexual aim is negatively understood as the removal of displeasure,' Miyasaki asserts, 'the instinct's relation to the object can only be active, and the object's relation to the instinct can only be passive. The instinct does not (and by definition cannot) *receive* pleasurable sensations from the object.' (ibid.) The achieved pleasure of the aim is the drive's 'own' action – the removal of an internal stimulus to the external world through the use (the means) of the object. Although the object as an occasion for the drive's activity is valuable, the object *as such* is almost irrelevant. As Laplanche (1976) succinctly puts it:

> Insofar as the object is that 'in which' the aim finds its realisation, the specificity or individuality of the object is, after all, of minimal concern; it is enough for it to possess certain *traits* which trigger the satisfying action; in itself, it remains relatively indifferent and contingent.
>
> (p. 12)

For Miyasaki, the consequences of Freud's position are disconcerting. The sexual relation of the drive to the object is, strictly speaking, no relation at all. This would seem to suggest that the sexual relation of subjects to one another is, likewise, no relation at all. Although individuals can serve simultaneously as an occasion for each other's pleasure, the satisfaction of one individual is independent of, and incidental to, that of the other as such. Each individual can only provide pleasure for the other as an object of that other individual's own activity, and not as an active subject. As Miyasaki states:

> The other is not an object of desire that the subject seeks to incor-
> porate or approach, but instead a painful external stimulus that
> heightens the internal stimulus of the instinctual source, necessitat-
> ing the repulsion of both sources of stimuli away from the subject.
> The moment of satisfaction is precisely the moment that the sexual
> other loses its utility and value as a means to that end.
>
> (p. 290)

So the 'masculinity' of the drive is not simply a matter, as Freud suggests, of the active nature of the drive. For Miyasaki, the Freudian 'drive' is masculine in the specifically heterosexual sense that it only relates to its object as to its contrary. It can only achieve satisfaction in a sexual object as passive, as the object upon which it acts. According to Miyasaki,

> [t]his view of the instinct seems to suggest that all forms of sexual
> relation, including non-heterosexual ones, must involve to some
> degree the oppositional roles of a positively defined masculine
> (the active achievement of pleasure) and a negatively defined
> feminine (the passive occasion for the removal of displeasure).
>
> (ibid.)

Clearly, the above view would present a problem, if Freud believed that the relations between individual subjects mirrored the relations of the drive to the sexual object. Obviously they do not, and Freud readily admits this. Thus, he attempts to locate instances where the subject also derives pleasure from the sexual object *as such*, and not only from the object's utility for the sexual aim. He believes that these instances are characteristic of what he calls 'object love'.

More specifically, in his paper 'On Narcissism: An Introduction' (1914), Freud begins by defining the notion of primary narcissism, namely, the initial investment of libido in the ego, an investment Freud termed 'ego-libido' and linked to 'the instinct of self-preservation' found in 'every living creature' (p. 74). As a component of ego development, primary narcissism governs the formation of later attachments to others, transforming ego-libido into what Freud called 'object-libido' (p. 76). In achieving a more developed type of selfhood, the subject forms attachments outside the self and constructs a self-image conditioned by an outside world of others and objects. The narcissistic constitution of subjectivity thus explains how human beings develop a sophisticated and realistic sense of self, realistic because their self-love yields to object-love and gives rise to an image of the self which can derive pleasure not just through an instrumental use of the object but though the appreciation of the value of the object *as such*. As he puts the issue, complete object-love

> displays the marked sexual *overvaluation* [my emphasis] which is doubtless derived from the child's original narcissism and thus corresponds to a transference of that narcissism to the sexual object.
>
> (p. 88)

It seems, therefore, that the sexual relation is not as tenuous as it appeared earlier. Overvaluation allows for a new perspective, by the subject, upon the sexual object's value. The object as such is not a matter of indifference (as Miyasaki claims), but is in every respect pleasurable.

However, Miyasaki argues that Freud's account of object-love does not sufficiently challenge the gender roles of sexual relation. He asserts that, although in this account the drive suffers somewhat in its 'masculinity' – in the broad sense of its 'activity' – and the subject does *receive* pleasure *passively* from the sexual object, the specific sense of masculinity – masculinity which relates to the other as to its opposite – is not severely damaged. While the subject has become both passive and active the object has not, by that fact, become active in the subject's eyes. As Miyasaki (2003) puts it:

> overvaluation does not, in fact, enable the subject to value the sexual object as such. The subject values the object in all of its aspects – but still as means to sexual pleasure. It overvalues the object only given its use for the sexual aim. If that utilitarian relation is upset, the ground of the object's overvaluation is lost.
>
> (p. 291)

This could also be deduced, Miyasaki suggests, from Freud's proposal that the need to cathect the object is created by an amount of drive stimulation that cannot be narcissistically satisfied. If the object does not satisfy this need by removing the excess excitation, then the motivation to preserve the bond with the object is removed. Consequently, overvaluation of the sexual object can only exist given the continued attachment of that object to the subject for the purpose of the sexual aim. The other cannot be valued in its absence to, or independence from, the subject.

For this reason, Miyasaki concludes that although object-love indicates an erotic bond, it still takes the form of a relation between opposites. The subject still takes pleasure only in the object's passive relation to its own activity. The subject needs and will form an attachment to a sexual object – but it does not value the sexual object as a subject. The fact that the object may also desire or receive pleasure is irrelevant to the subject's pleasure, which is always an object *qua* object. In this respect, Freud's account of object-love implies that the subject loves the object less for its uniqueness and separateness, and more for its ability to contract the subject's own abundance, that is, to embody and reflect back that part of itself it has invested in the object.

It is not surprising, therefore, that in the same paper (i.e., 'On Narcissism – An Introduction') Freud perceives object-love as a predominantly male affair. More specifically, Freud believes that, whereas women tend to be narcissistic in their love, men have a propensity to transfer their narcissism from themselves to the object of their love. It is this process that leads to the 'overvaluation' of their love object. Freud is thinking here of the love-struck man who cannot take his eyes of his beloved. In the throes of this feverish state, the masculine sense of self is weakened by being utterly absorbed in eroticized contemplation of the beloved. In order to restore his self's narcissistic integrity, therefore, the man's externalized, projected narcissism needs to be returned by the beloved. In other words, the beloved has to passively embody and reflect back man's active projection of his own narcissism. If his narcissism is not returned, then the object has to be abandoned and replaced with a new one. What Freud seems to suggest here is that men, in their attempt to obtain narcissistic fulfilment from the object, necessarily fail to appreciate the uniqueness and irreplaceability of the object of their love.

Clewell's critique of Freud's account of mourning

It is this account of the (masculine) subject's narcissistic relation to the object that Tammy Clewell (2004) also identifies as problematic in Freud's analysis of the process of mourning in 'Mourning and Melancholia' (1917). In this paper, Freud portrays the loss of a love object as a temporary disruption of the mourner's narcissism. Restoring the subject to itself thus depends on a rather straightforward process of abandoning emotional ties, repudiating the lost other, and assimilating the loss to a consoling substitute. The self is restored and the work of mourning brought to a decisive close, Freud believes, when the free libido has been reinvested in a new object. As a process of detachment and disavowal,

Clewell claims, Freud's mourning theory follows his general theory of the 'masculine' activity of the drive (and the subject) which can only be maintained at the expense of the object's separateness and well-being, a theory in which the subject neutralizes the enduring pain of loss by realizing the irrelevance of the lost object for its own satisfaction and accepting consolation in the form of a substitute for what has been lost.

However, Clewell asserts that Freud's later account of mourning in *The Ego and the Id* (1923) significantly challenges his earlier one. More specifically, in this work, Freud re-examines the dynamics of melancholic identification and admits that he 'did not appreciate the full significance of this process and did not know how common and how typical it is' (Freud, 1923, p. 28). What he now understands is that the identification process previously linked to a pathological failure to mourn (i.e., melancholia) provides 'the sole condition under which the id can give up its objects' (ibid., p. 29). During the early stage of human development, the infant negotiates the loss of or separation from a primary love object by identifying with the lost other. Identification thus becomes the condition for constituting the self, giving rise to a psyche internally divided as ego, id and superego. It is only by internalizing the lost other through the work of bereaved identification, Freud now claims, that one becomes a subject in the first place.

According to Clewell, therefore, this account of mourning substantially revises our understanding of what it means to work through a loss. As she puts it:

> Working through no longer entails abandoning the object and reinvesting the free libido in a new one; it no longer entails accepting consolation in the form of an external substitute for the loss, as Freud had postulated in 'Mourning and Melancholia'. Rather, working through depends on taking the lost other into the structure of one's own identity, a form of preserving the lost object in and as the self.
>
> (Clewell, 2004, p. 61)

Correspondingly, as the internalized lost object becomes a necessary condition for the establishment of one's own sense of self, Freud's account of the 'masculine' nature of the drive and the subject which only relates to its object as to its opposite is drastically undermined.

Yet, Clewell astutely observes that, despite his undermining of the 'masculine' constitution of the subject, Freud still believes that identification with the rival object (rather than the lost love object) governs 'normal' subject formation. For example, in his discussion of the 'simple positive Oedipus complex in a boy', which is characterized by an 'ambivalent attitude to his father and an object-relation of a solely affectionate kind to his mother' (Freud, 1923, p. 32), Freud claims that in negotiating the loss of the mother, the boy replaces this maternal object cathexis 'by one of two things: either an identification with his mother or an intensification of his identification with his father' (ibid., p. 32). Freud does acknowledge the possibility of the former mode of identification by suggesting the boy may identify with the lost maternal other; however, he renders this option an exception to the general rule in claiming that we 'are accustomed to regard the latter outcome as the more normal' (ibid., p. 32). Even when the discussion moves on to 'the more complete Oedipus complex, which is twofold, positive and negative' (ibid., p. 33) and thus includes the boy's object-cathexis to his father, Freud continues to imply that identification with the rival, in this case the mother, constitutes the norm.

In order to offset Freud's prioritization of a type of identification which promotes an antagonistic relation to the object, Clewell identifies certain notions in Freud's work that question this primacy. Thus, in a major challenge to the notion of rivalrous identification at the foundation of his account of the Oedipus complex, Freud claims that the ambivalence displayed in the relations to the parents should be attributed entirely to bisexuality and 'that it is not ... developed out of identification in consequence of rivalry' (Freud, 1923, p. 33). Thus, Clewell avers that

> when Freud goes on to speculate that ambivalent feelings for the father, as for the mother in the negative Oedipus Complex, may have nothing to do with rivalry, his work suggests that we can no longer interpret ambivalence as deriving from the outside, as blamed on the contesting other.... Rather, ambivalence may be understood as an effect of the very separation between self and other, as the product of bereaved internalisation. Identification with the lost other, establishes the condition for founding the self and, hence, constituting internal divisions within the psyche. In this sense identification simultaneously creates and frustrates a desire for fusion or unity of selfhood. ... [I]n recognizing there can be no final severance of attachments without dissolving the ego, Freud's late theory suggests a different alternative: the mourning subject may affirm the endurance of ambivalent bonds to those loved and lost others as a condition of its own existence.
>
> (Clewell, 2004, pp. 64–5)

Clewell believes, therefore, that Freud's work counsels us to relinquish the wish for a strict, narcissistic/masculinistic identity unencumbered by the claims of the lost other or the past. In so doing, it helps us to establish 'an intimate, indeed ethical, relation between past and future, as we embark on the present work of *endless mourning* [my emphasis]' (ibid., p. 65).

Defending Freud's position

Clewell's praise of Freud's emphasis on 'endless mourning' as an antidote to the fixity of self-identity produced by the rivalrous identification with the other and Miyasaki's critique of the dominance of a 'masculine', narcissistic perspective in Freud's conception of the drive are deeply problematic as they misrepresent Freud's initial intentions in the following five ways.

First, despite his problematic characterization of the drive as 'masculine', Freud's actual distinction between the drive's sexual aim and the sexual object is introduced as part of his overall attempt to challenge our belief in the existence of a fixed, predetermined heterosexual link between the two. The assumption of a necessary heterosexual connection is so unwarranted, he claims, that 'the exclusive sexual interest felt by men for women is a problem that needs elucidation' (Freud, 1905, p. 146 ft). Nor does he distinguish individuals according to gender: 'Pure masculinity or femininity is not to be found either in a psychological or a biological sense' (Freud, 1905, p. 220 ft). To argue, therefore, (as Miyasaki does) that Freud's view of the 'masculine' quality of the drive indicates his fundamental heterosexist stance towards all sexual relations is to disregard Freud's revolutionary insights regarding the 'anarchic', 'polymorphous perverse' nature of human sexuality.

Second, the absence of a predetermined connection between the subject's erotic activity and its object does not necessary imply that the subject's cathexis of the object can be *easily* revoked whenever the object fails to provide satisfaction to the subject. It usually takes a series of grave disappointments and a long process of mourning for this bond to be severed. Moreover, the creation and establishment of a solid, durable bond between the subject and the object is absolutely crucial for the former's well-being. As Freud puts it: 'A strong egoism is a protection against disease, but in the last resort we must begin to love in order that we may not fall ill' (Freud, 1914, p. 66).

Moreover, Freud's replacement of the sexual drive by Eros in *Beyond the Pleasure Principle* (1920) makes the erotic bond with the other even more crucial for both our survival and well-being. If, according to Freud's thesis, the living substance goes to death by an inner movement, what fights against death is not something internal to life, but the conjugation of two mortal substances. Eros is precisely this conjugation; the desire of the other is directly implied in the emergence of Eros; it is always with another that the living substance fights against death, against its own death, whereas when it acts separately it pursues death through the circuitous paths of adaptation to the natural and cultural environment. Freud does not look for the drive for life in some *will to live* inscribed in each living substance: in the living substance *by itself* he finds only death. There is almost a reversal of the active and passive roles of drive and object here: if the ultimate aim of all drives is the return to the eternal 'passivity' of inorganic matter, what keeps us alive and 'active' is our relationship with the other/object.

Third, both Miyasaki and Clewell unreservedly assume that Freud presents primary narcissism as an objectless state. Certain theorists (e.g., Laplanche (1976), Green (2001) and Cohen (2005, 2007)), however, argue that Freud had also from the outset conceived the narcissistic position as conditioned by the relation to the object. For these theorists, the most sustained development of this insight is to be found in the last part of 'On Narcissism: An Introduction' itself where Freud writes:

> If we look at the attitude of affectionate parents toward their children, we have to recognise that it is a revival and reproduction of their own narcissism, which they have long since abandoned. ... The child ... shall once more really be the centre and core of creation – 'His Majesty the Baby', as we once fancied ourselves. The child shall fulfil those wishful dreams of the parents which they never carried out.
>
> (Freud 1914, pp. 90–1)

What Freud seems to imply in the above extract is that narcissism comes into being only by way of the detour of the parents' projections, so that the child can locate its centre in itself only through such projections. As Laplanche puts it, 'It is in terms of parental omnipotence, experienced as such by the child, and of its introjection, that the megalomania and the narcissistic state of the child may be understood' (p. 79). The sovereignty of 'His Majesty' can be constituted and affirmed only by the love of its parents. Self-love, therefore, is always also the introjected love of the other. In this respect, Freud implicitly deconstructs the sharp distinction between narcissism and object-love since, for both men and women, there can be no object-love without narcissism and there can be no narcissism without object-love, that is to say, 'narcissism which does not enforce and is enforced by the love of the other' (Cohen, 2005, p. 94). (A similar argument regarding the Freudian notion of 'narcissism' can be found in L. O'Carroll's 'On Men's Friendship With Other Men', Chapter 6 in this book).

Fourth, it is doubtful whether Clewell's commendation of the work of 'endless mourning' establishes an intimate, ethical relation to the lost object and the past. On the contrary, it fosters the illusion of permanence of the object that Freud would do so much to undermine. For example, in his 1916 paper 'On Transience' Freud argues that it is impermanence that confers value to the object; it is the realization of the transient nature of the object that creates pleasure. The wishful fantasy of everlasting relation to the object is itself an attack on the possibility of pleasure, a wish to render the experience of pleasure redundant. Love at its strongest, Freud implies, is an acknowledgement of transience, not an obstinate denial of it.

This appreciation of transience, Freud claims, is the outcome of one's attitude to mourning. Inability (or unwillingness) to mourn leads to fear of loving, which amounts for Freud to an inability to live. Those in this position, he writes, like people after the war,

> seem ready to make a permanent renunciation because what was precious has proved not to be lasting, [they] are simply in a state of mourning for what is lost. Mourning, as we know, however painful it may be, comes to a spontaneous end. When it has renounced everything that has been lost, then it has consumed itself, and our libido is once more free (in so far as we are still young and active) to replace the lost objects by fresh ones equally or still more precious.
>
> (Freud, 1916, p. 98)

Freud's intent here is extremely clear. Refusal to mourn is refusal to live. Mourning is the necessary suffering that makes more life possible. But it does require of us not only an ability to mourn, but also the larger capacity to mourn the whole notion of permanence.

But there is also a contradiction in Freud's reasoning. More life is only possible if we can let ourselves mourn; and yet, he says, those who renounce life (and love) are in a perpetual state of mourning. Perhaps those eternal mourners (like Clewell) have transferred their loyalty from the permanent to mourning itself. As if they are trying to convince themselves, that if nothing else lasts, mourning can. This, one could say, is how intractable the belief in permanence has become through all its time-honoured reinforcements. The continuity of one's life, the unfailing certainty, could be mourning. Thus, as Adam Philips states:

> Good mourning, in Freud's terms, keeps people moving on, keeps them in time; bad mourning becomes something akin to an ascetic personal religion. It is impossible to love life, Freud intimates, without loving transience. Religion shores promises against our unavoidable ruin. So 'successful' mourning that comes to a 'spontaneous end' is secular. It is, in other words, open-ended, a restoring of appetite. And the open-ended is Freud's shorthand definition of the new secular world. Appetite moves us by moving on.
>
> (Philips, 1999, p. 28)

Moreover, Freud's later theory of mourning does not necessarily contradict his initial one. On the contrary, it amplifies it by introducing elements that make it more complex. Perhaps one way of looking at this is that, for Freud, it is still a matter of great significance to leave significant objects behind in the outside world, but we can only do this by carrying them on with us inside our ego. As we are getting older, the ego expands as those external objects that are significant to us become fewer and fewer. However, this process of mourning is not an endless one. It still comes to a spontaneous end when we are ready to accept the loss of these objects as ideal, that is to say, by acknowledging them not as omnipotent and permanent but as potent and transient. In other words, by mourning the loss of a succession of 'ideal objects' – the ideal mother, the ideal self, the ideal father, etc. – we replace them by internal symbolizations which allow us to recognize that neither we nor anyone else ever was or ever could be everlasting, omnipresent and omnipotent.

Finally, Freud's prioritization of Oedipal identification is inseparable from his appreciation of transience and the process of mourning. The boy identifies with the father as a rival at the same time as he separates himself from him in order to create his own place. There is no doubt that the figure of the Oedipal father is intrinsically violent as he threatens the son with sanctions and demands from him to renounce his desires so as to conform to the existing societal principles. However, his authority is also unique because it is grounded in negativity: the Oedipal father exercises his authority in the belief that he can lose it. He presents the son with his authority but he also lets him know that he can displace him, put his authority to the trial of death.

By presenting his authority as a transient force, therefore, the father enables his son to mourn the loss of an ideal, omnipotent paternal figure as he realizes that there is no father who has absolute power, who cannot *potentially* become dead. Moreover, by positing himself as envious of the place of the father, desirous of occupying his place, the son assumes this place and is being put to the trial of death himself, for, of course, if he puts himself in the place of the father, he risks being subjected to the same hazards he inflicts. In other words, this Oedipal scenario does not only enable the son to question the father's authority, it also enables him to deconstruct the paternal/patriarchal legacy that lives on within him. By carrying out this double task, the son is able to go through the emotional pain of recognizing that neither he nor his father (nor any other man) ever was or ever could be an ideal, perfect, God-like being. Moreover, this realization provides the son with the opportunity to witness the damage that is caused by the violence underpinning the assumption of an omnipotent paternal position and attempt to live, not in some imagined patriarchal heaven, but in a better, more egalitarian, world so as to avoid inflicting this damage on others.

But what happens when the father is unable to allow his son to put his authority to the trial of death because he is forced to renounce it altogether by contemporary social forces which humiliate him? Would the son become incapable of challenging him and seek alternative identifications with more powerful, God-like paternal figures? Or, would he be required to abandon his search for autonomy by melancholically identifying with the father's lost authority? Indeed, these seem to be the outcomes of our current social environment which does not know the Oedipus complex, but only the slaying of the father. Such a climate produces a belated and remorseful understanding with one's father, similar to the one between condemned prisoners. The societal violence which is inflicted on the father makes the son forget the violence the father committed.

Consequently, the son is afraid to clash with his father because, first, the father, as a result of the severe societal blows he has received, has become so fragile that he is unable to withstand his son's attacks and, second, the only victory the son has to look forward to is a hollow one as the only thing that it guarantees is his survival in a world that is far worse than the merely bad represented by the father. It seems as if the oppressive function of the father was simultaneously the nourishing germ-cell of the son's unbending will for a different one. What disintegrates today along with the function of the father is not just the most effective agency of the bourgeoisie, but also the resistance which, though repressing the son's individuality, also strengthened, perhaps even produced it.

What we are advocating here, however, is not a nostalgic, uncritical return to the Oedipal father for what he mainly demanded was the son's submission to the abstract centres of bourgeois control, and the questioning of this last required a revolt against the father's repressive function. However, this revolt did not change the existing social structure or improve the father–son relation but led to the demolition of the father which simultaneously made the son's psychological constitution that much more susceptible to social control and eliminated any constructive elements of individual resistance (for a more detailed discussion of the decline of the father's power and its effects on the son's identity formation, see my paper 'The Phantom of the Primal Father', Chapter 5 in this book).

Conclusion

To sum up: in their attempt to deconstruct stereotypical gender distinctions and establish a different, ethical relationship between the 'masculine' subject and its 'feminine' object/other, both Miyasaki and Clewell misinterpret Freud's notions of the drive, narcissism, object love, and the process of mourning. This is because they fail to appreciate the complexity of Freud's ideas and how they illuminate the really existing relations between men and women, fathers and sons and not stop at their abstraction. More specifically, his views allow men to perceive how their lives can only be sustained and nourished through their active engagement with the other, how current social structures force them to seek refuge in non-activity, and how their 'praxis' in this world contracts to an endless, passive observation of the destruction of both their self and the other. In this way, it is possible to use his ideas so as to understand and change their current alienating social environment.

5
The Phantom of the Primal Father

Anastasios Gaitanidis

In this chapter, I aim to examine why the notion of the 'primal father' introduced in *Totem and Taboo* (1913) was so important to Freud, how it has been received by subsequent psychoanalysts, how it seems to have been completely rejected by anthropological research, but also how it can still contribute to the formation of an explanatory framework that can help us understand the problems arising from the diminishing significance of the father in the formation of masculine identity.

The Freudian account of the primal father

Freud gives a fundamental place to the role of the father in his configuration of the trajectory of a subject who is shot through with his desires and dreams but limited in his passions by the sanction of the law. But he also realizes that this role is in decline as it has been undermined by the mounting power of irreversible social changes. The rise of modernity has contributed to the creation of the autonomous, sovereign individual which has helped to bring about a slow but steady deterioration of the centuries-old power and status of the paternal authority. For Freud, this modern situation is fundamentally Oedipal, that is to say, the basic dynamics of the Oedipus complex, while certainly not limited to the modern age, are specifically intensified by the Oedipal rebellion against paternal authority that characterizes the modern condition.

However, he also realizes that patriarchal authority, though under attack, is by no means dead. Indeed, precisely because it is under attack, new affirmations of patriarchal authority are more ruthless than ever. Far from it being the case that modernity has brought about the decline of patriarchy, its influence has given rise to forms of political reaction which resist this decline and seek to install a renewed dominion of paternal authority. Although most of Freud's work can be perceived as an attempt to theorize the individual and social effects of this simultaneous dethroning and revalorization of paternal authority, it is in *Totem and Taboo* (1913) that these effects are clearly illuminated with the aid of Darwin's hypothesis of the primal horde. Here it is in outline:

In primitive times, people lived in small hordes, each of them under the despotic sway of a male – the primal father – who appropriated all the females to himself. If any of the sons tried to usurp his privileges and possess the females, he attacked them and killed them, or drove them off, or reduced them to abject submission. Those who were driven off no doubt tried to capture females from the horde or other hordes to set up groups of their own. Those who remained did so on the condition of controlling and repressing their desires towards their father's wives. The repressed libido was diverted to strengthen the ties between them and bind them into a unity. United they were able to do what singly they had all wanted to do but had lacked the power to carry out. They killed and devoured the father.

After this murder, however, the brothers were seized with guilt and a need to atone. The guilt was a result of the tender feelings for the father. Behind the hate was love. This led to proscribing the killing of the totem and to the deification of the father as the totem animal of the tribe, an animal whose life was sacred except at special feast occasions when he was sacrificed and the ancient crime was symbolically relived. But also the brothers feared each other. The danger was that there would be competition among them to see who would take the father's place and repeat the subjugation of the rest. The only way to avoid this repetition was to continue to accept the veto imposed by the father during his lifetime. The women of the horde – or tribe as it becomes – had to be taboo to them and they sought their wives from outside groups (i.e., both the incest taboo and exogamy were introduced at the same time). The dead father was as powerful as when he was alive. He endured in their minds as an idea, an image or a symbol, imposing the unbreakable laws (see Freud 1912–13, Ch. 4).

In some such way as this, Freud suggests, the primal father image persisting in the minds of the males of the tribe became the source of tribal law and psychologically was the chief instrument in enforcing it. This image, however, did not only endure in the minds of the tribal males but has become embodied in the inherited structure of the mind as at least a nucleus upon which children's fantasies of the real father are constructed, fantasies whose aggressivity exceeds what, according to Freud, is 'currently justified'. This rage, disproportionate as it is to the aggression perpetrated against the child by the real father is, however, commensurate with the aggression of the primal father, who was 'undoubtedly terrible' in his aggressiveness towards his children. Hence the horrible aggression of the primal father engendered an equally horrible aggression from the sons, and this patricidal aggression, repeated many times in prehistory, established a fund of aggressivity on which modern children draw when they make the first excessive 'instalment' on the aggressivity of their own superegos by overreacting to parental prohibition and then turning the energy of this overreaction against themselves (see Freud, 1930, Ch. 7).

It seems, therefore, that this excessive aggressivity that is characteristic of children's fantasies of their real father is the evidence that Freud uses to support the need to put forward the hypothesis of the murder of the primal father. However, one cannot help but wonder just what amount of aggressivity is 'justified' in a small child's reaction to parental prohibition. Is it possible to *objectively* determine the excessiveness of this aggressivity? And if there is no way of determining whether the child's aggressivity is excessive, how then can it serve as a justification for Freud's insistence on the actuality of the murder of the primal father?

However, despite the lack of any objective validation, one can still argue that the child's excessive aggressivity could be seen to exist as a necessary *logical* outcome of Freud's (1923) suggestion that the child's superego originates not from the identification with the real father but with the father's superego which, in turn, originates from the identification with his father's superego and so on and so forth. This eventually (and logically) takes us back to a primary historical event which is responsible for the formation of the first superego, that is, the brothers' introjection of the prohibitions of the dead primal father. The upshot of this retrospective account, therefore, is that this initial introjection is a necessary part of all subsequent superego formations. Thus, if the child's superego is mainly formed through this initial introjection (of the harsh prohibitions of the dead primal father) then the absence of a rectilinear connection between the severity of the child's superego and the real severity of the father appears to be justifiable.

However, the real difficulty with the above argument, according to Laplanche and Pontalis (1986), is not its lack of empirical validation or its logical plausibility/ implausibility but its reliance on Freud's genetic method, 'his search for chronology, going backwards into time towards the first real, verifiable elements' (p. 15). This method is the product of Freud's unwillingness to resign himself to treating fantasy as the pure and simple outgrowth of the spontaneous psychic life of the infant.

For him the psychical reality of fantasy must ultimately be based on the ground of reality. Thus, he assumes the existence of *Urszenen* (primal scenes), true scenes in early infancy that determine the later development of fantasy. In his case history of the Wolf Man, 'one is struck by the passionate conviction that urges Freud, like a detective on a watch, to establish the reality of the scene (the observation of the parental intercourse) down to its smallest details' (Laplanche and Pontalis, 1986, p. 16). But here his doubts are coming up again: must there necessarily occur such an event in every childhood? In reply to this question he introduces the notion of *Urphantasien* (primal fantasies) which inevitably leads to another question: where do these fantasies come from? They are mnemic residues transmitted hereditarily from actual, 'real' experiences in the history of the human species. In Freud's own words: 'all the things that are told to us today in analysis as fantasy ... were once real occurrences in the primaeval times of the human family' (1916–17, p. 371).

However, in making the leap from fantasy to historical reality, Freud forgets what he himself discovered – that all reality undergoes modification upon entering the unconscious – and is thus misled into positing such factual events as the murder of the father by the primal horde. It is this short-circuit between reality and the unconscious which, first, undermines the productive power of the unconscious and, second, lends these events their mythical character. The positing of such events has served to reinforce the resistances of anthropological research that has no trouble of disproving their empirical plausibility.

The Lacanian account of the primal father

For certain theorists, it is precisely the mythical character of the hypothesis of the murder of the primal father that is its most attractive feature. One of the most prominent theorists, Jacques Lacan (1992), regards the empirical implausibility of the primordial murder of the father as a virtue of Freud's thesis because this murder, as mythical, can be assigned to that no-place and no-time that is the transcendent locus of the Law (which for Lacan is always the Law-of-the-Father, i.e., patriarchal Law). More specifically, Lacan argues that Freud taught us to recognize, in the murder of the primal father, the primordial event which inaugurates the symbolic debt binding each subject to the Law. This myth of the primordial killing of the father describes how ethical humanity is constituted by a relation of infinite guilt towards a vanished figure (i.e., the primal father), such that the destructive aggressivity of the subject is channelled back against itself through the circuit of love and guilt that the crime against the primal father activates. The primal father is dead, yet the place of his disappearance marks the locus of the debt and the obligation to which the Law holds us hostage. In other words, although the primal father is dead, his phantom – that is, his Law – still haunts us.

Moreover, as this phantom/Law emanates from the empty place of the vanished figure of the primal father, it is impossible for any real father to occupy this place – that is, to be the Law. He can only be the *representative* of the Law. However, as he cannot pronounce the Law in his own name, the Law can never be directly present for us. We always find ourselves, in other words, 'before the Law', the Law itself continually eluding us (for a similar argument, see Derrida, 1985). Thus, the ultimate origin of the Law always withdraws. There is no possibility of catching a glimpse of the Law itself. Its origin – like that of any phantom – can then be expressed only in a mythical way. From a Lacanian point of view, therefore, Freud formulates a mythical story of origins which supplies an answer to the question of the origin of the Law. Any empirical interpretation of this myth then becomes an obstacle preventing us from understanding the transcendental status of the Law.

But what happens if the Law has ceased to be considered as transcendent and has been assigned a worldly locus? This immanent concretization of the Law could potentially obstruct and endanger our ethical relation to the socio-political order. Indeed, according to Joan Copjec (1996), an important neo-Lacanian theorist, if the Law is understood as immanent, then the ethical imperative that places a limit on the assimilation of the other is annulled. It is this imperative that prevents us from assuming the position of a totalitarian (super)-subject. After all, democracy originates from and on the basis of an ethical respect for what makes totalization (the absolute immanence of the Law) impossible. It is respect for this impossibility. Thus, the Law must always be set out of the reach of appropriation for the ends of those whose real wish is to pervert the command of the Law. The myth of the primordial murder of the father, therefore, provides us with an adequate representation of the transcendent character of the Law, 'causing us', as Copjec (1996) says, 'to respect a father with whom we are unable to identify and a law to which we are unable to conform' (p. xxii).

While the above position is fascinating and provocative, one should not subscribe to it fully. This is because it supports the view that opacity – that is, the impossibility of locating the origin of the Law – is an irreducible feature of sociality as such. Such a view is explicit in Lacan's (and his followers') insistence that we should accept the notion of legality as an irreducible 'given' which constitutes in advance the possibility of socialization. Whereas particular laws may be social products, this Law cannot be a social product. It is, rather, an irreducible violence (exemplified by the murder of the primal father), an imposition which is always already the precondition for any sociality whatever. It is just the transcendental status of this kind of gesture which is problematic. It establishes the Law as a *de facto* invariant devoid of any historical and sociological content.

Castoriadis's critique of the Lacanian account of the primal father

It is not surprising, therefore, that Lacan and his followers have been characterized by certain theorists as being historically and sociologically blind. For instance, Castoriadis (1997) argues that when Lacanians read the myth of *Totem and Taboo*, they see only the murder of the father and ignore the oath of the brothers who swear not to kill each other and not to want, each for himself, all the women of the horde. For Castoriadis, this alliance is paradigmatic of any democratic society where the power of the father is limited by the power of the other fathers, and not just by an impersonal Law. As he puts it:

> The father refers to an instituted collectivity by means of a law, and it is a living collectivity that limits his power. Otherwise one would have a child who would forever be slave to the father, or his enemy, eaten up by inextinguishable feelings of hatred. The assumption of a filial relationship cannot occur unless one assimilates the idea of the father's limitation, the fact that the father is one father among other fathers.
>
> (Castoriadis, 1997, p. 188)

Moreover, one must also assimilate that there is something – the collectivity and its institution – that is more general and that goes beyond him. However, in positing the empty place of the dead primal father as the transcendental locus of the Law, Lacan and his followers abstract from the specific historical constitution of democratic law an account which is totally unconnected with any living, concrete collectivity (for a thorough discussion of Castoriadis's psychological and sociological positions, See O'Carroll's 'Achieving Our Country: Ethnic Difference and White Men's Racism', Chapter 9 in this book).

Nonetheless, although Castoriadis rightly criticizes the abstract/ transcendental nature of the Lacanian interpretation of the murder of the primal father, he emphasizes only the aspect of this myth (i.e., the brothers' alliance) that has a concrete application to every living collectivity. In other words, by shifting the focus of attention away from the murder of the primal father and onto the establishment of a strong alliance between the brothers, Castoriadis prematurely assumes that the concept of the primal father is an abstraction which does not have any application whatsoever.

A dialectical account of the primal father

The upshot of the above discussion is that one should not rush either to hypostatize the notion of the primal father by abstracting it from its concrete socio-historical basis and regarding it as the transcendental locus of an opaque, phantom-like Law or to jettison it *tout court* because one cannot find any immediate, concrete applications for it. On the contrary, one should view this Freudian concept as a *real abstraction* – that is, an abstract social moment which asserts itself at precisely the deepest stratum of the concrete individual. One finds here, therefore, a dialectical motif in Freud's account of the murder of primal father. This motif lies in the fact that Freud made the discovery that the more deeply one explores the phenomena of human individuation, the more unreservedly one grasps the individual as a self-contained and dynamic entity, the closer one draws to that in the individual which is really no longer individual. This can be given a far more general, philosophical twist, by saying that the dialectic of the particular and the general (as taught by Hegel), with the sense that the particular is the general and the general the particular, can be rediscovered in Freud's project against the grain of its psychological intentions. For Freud came up against the fact that the innermost core on which the psychology of the single individual rests is itself something general, namely, certain very general – though admittedly archaic – structures of the social context in which individuals are contained. This dialectical quality of the notion of the primal father calls for further clarification.

As it has already been mentioned above, Freud's work was engendered by the decline of the paternal function as an attempt to illuminate the effects of this decline via a theory centred on the figure of Oedipus. In this Oedipal model, the son takes over the role of the father by identifying with him, develops a conception of self and wins autonomy. In this situation whatever autonomy the son achieves develops 'with and against the father'. But with the massive socio-economic changes that have occurred during the period of late modernity, this process has radically altered.

More specifically, in the early phases of his development the son still undergoes the same experiences of hate and love with respect to his father which constituted the Oedipus complex. More rapidly than before, however, the son discovers that the father by no means embodies the power, justice and goodness the son had initially expected. The actual weakness of the father within society affects the formation of the son's superego: he can no longer identify with the father, no longer can accomplish that internalization of the paternal demands, which with all their repressive moments still contributed decisively to the formation of an autonomous individual. Therefore, there is today actually no longer the conflict between the powerful father and the son's no less powerful ego; instead the two, equally weak are split apart. From his relationship to his father, the son now carries away only the abstract idea of arbitrary, unconditional power and strength and then searches for a stronger, more powerful father than the real one, who is truly adequate to this image, a primal father. This transformation of the father–son relation also provides us with an explanation for Freud's aforementioned view that the son's superego originates not from the identification with the real father but with the father's superego whose origins can be traced back to the initial internalization of the prohibitions of the primal father (for a more extensive exposition of this thesis, see Institute of Social Research, 1973).

This search for a more powerful, primal father has far-reaching socio-political consequences that can be detected in Freud's (1921) analysis of group dynamics in *Group Psychology and the Analysis of the Ego*. In this text, Freud argues that, by regressing to the position of the primal horde, a group of men replace their internalized ego-ideals – which, as we mentioned above, are frail as a result of the weakened position of the real father in a crisis-leaden unstable economy – with a common ego-ideal which they find embodied in a charismatic leader who figures as the all-powerful primal father. Literally hypnotized by this figure, this group of men internalize his demands and make them their own.

The psychological mechanism which allows this to happen is that of primary identification (for a detailed definition of 'primary identification', see Laplanche and Pontalis, 1983). For Freud this identification is 'the earliest expression of an emotional tie with another person,' playing 'a part in the early history of the Oedipus complex' (Freud, 1921, p. 60). This primary identification helps to bring about the separation of the leader image as that of an all-powerful primal father from the actual father image. Since a man's identification with his real father as an answer to the Oedipus complex is only a secondary phenomenon, infantile regression may go beyond the already weakened father image and through an *anaclitic* ('leaning on') process reach a more archaic one (for a detailed definition of *anaclisis*, see Laplanche and Pontalis, 1983).

Moreover, this primary identification always presupposes a narcissistic appropriation: as the ego identifies with the object and places it inside itself, object-cathexis gives way to a strangely ambivalent love of the self. On the one hand, each man in the group is gratified by the feeling the identification gives of 'aggrandisement', of belonging to something 'bigger' than oneself. On the other hand, since the leader image appears omnipotent due to its collusion with the archaic father-image of the primal horde, it is only possible to have a masochistic attitude towards it. Thus, each man in the group not only loves and reveres authority, he also fears and hates it. Exploiting the mechanism of this primary identification and the gratification it offers, this group of men develops what Freud (1920) calls 'a thirst for obedience' (p. 76).

Additionally, the hypothesis of the primal father and his relationship to the members of the primal horde throws light not only on this group's unqualified obedience to the authority of the group leader, but also on the relationships between the men in the group. According to Freud, the primary jealousy that exists between the members of the psychological 'brother horde' can be counterbalanced only by their similar love for the same object, that is, the introjected primal father-figure: thus their coherence should be interpreted as a reaction formation, resulting in ambivalence, against their mutual aggression. But this defensive manoeuvre (like any defensive strategy) will eventually break down and the cohesiveness of this group of men will be under threat. A direct outlet of these men's covert aggression needs to be found: their negative emotions need to be projected upon the out-group. Thus, the members of the out-group must become scapegoats whose sacrifice satisfies the unconscious wish to inflict harm on the other men of the in-group (for a more detailed presentation of this argument, see Adorno (1951) in Arato and Gebhardt, 1978).

Consequently, Freud's analysis of group dynamics on the basis of the relation of the primal father to the primal horde can be used to explain how the current social changes in the construction of fatherhood have produced a masculine identity which is obedient to external authority and aggressive towards members of the out-group. Without this analysis, we would not be able to comprehend how countless groups of men constantly engage in acts of unimaginable violence towards others.

A case example

Let me illustrate the usefulness of the Freudian analysis mentioned above by providing a brief description of one of my own clinical cases. Jack, a 35-year-old man, started therapy with me because he suffered from depression. During his childhood, he felt closer to his father than to his mother, whom he initially perceived as having been distant and aloof. However, when Jack was 11 years old, his father went bankrupt and subsequently experienced a long period of depression (3 years) which eventually led him to abandon his wife and son. Jack was devastated by this abandonment and felt betrayed by his father (who also did not make any effort to keep in touch with him over the years). This had reinforced his ambivalence towards men who occupied positions of authority such as his boss, me, and so on. He felt, on the one hand, the desire to be protected and guided by these figures and, on the other, the need to protect himself against their potential betrayal and abandonment.

Jack tried to secure his financial future by becoming a public servant and avoiding financial risks. However, he had recently been made redundant due to the massive job cuts in the public sector. He was extremely angry with the UK government, in general, and his manager, in particular, for not securing his position and not giving him adequate notice so as to find another job. Yet, he was unable to express his anger as he felt he could not achieve anything by doing this. This powerlessness made him feel increasingly depressed and he was afraid that he would end up being like his father. In an attempt to overcome this fear and his increased helplessness and passivity, he decided to join (while he was in therapy) an extreme right-wing political group which was led by a man who, according to Jack, was very strong and 'charismatic'. Jack revealed that, for the first time in his life, he was able to find some 'hope' and 'meaning' by realizing that he could rely on this leader and his political group. He could 'see' now that this leader was right to insist that the recent financial crisis was due to the greed of 'Jewish bankers' who had to be 'stopped' before they completely destroyed his country. He also realized that the rise in unemployment was due to the increasing number of immigrants who were allowed to work in this country. Of course, he emphasized that he had no problems with immigrants like me who were 'educated' and 'sophisticated', but he believed that all the 'other' immigrants should be immediately deported and their jobs should be given back to honest, hard-working citizens like him.

It was obvious that the leader of this group served as a substitute for Jack's unattained ideals. He trusted him on account of the perfections which he had striven to reach for his own self, and which he now liked to procure in this roundabout way as a means of satisfying his self-worth. By making this 'charismatic' leader his ideal, Jack loved himself, as it were, and got rid of the stains of passivity, powerlessness and discontent which marred his picture of his own empirical self. This pattern of identification through idealization of the leader also gratified Jack's twofold wish to submit to authority and to be an authority himself.

Throughout our therapeutic work, I felt very uncomfortable with Jack's political views and his 'idealization' of this leader and his group. However, I kept reminding myself that Jack's political choice was irrational as it was based on his need to defend himself against his vulnerability and sense of powerlessness. I also realized that Jack was feeling very angry with me for not occupying the position of the 'expert' who would provide him with the answers he needed. In contrast to the leader of the group, I did not give him any clear directions or explanations and, for this reason, I was sometimes perceived as a 'weak' and abandoning paternal figure. However, despite his frustration and anger with me, Jack did not terminate his therapy as he was aware that I was a consistent, reliable presence in his life and I was able to deeply understand his emotional turmoil. This allowed me to invite Jack to express his anger about my perceived 'weakness' and reflect on his tendency to initially idealize and then become disappointed with paternal/authority figures. This also enabled him to express his anger towards his father and reconcile it with the love he felt for him. In other words, as Jack was able to gradually withstand the ambivalent feelings he had for me, he begun to modify his view of his father, forgive his vulnerability and weakness and deal with the disappointment he felt with him. Of course, this also helped him to become more accepting of his own vulnerability and weakness and to perceive this acceptance as a sign of strength.

More importantly, however, Jack begun to realize that it was the fear of his own vulnerability and his need to defend against it that transformed the leader of the group into a God-like figure. Thus, he became progressively disillusioned with this leader and his group. He also realized that, just as little as he believed in the depth of his heart that the Jewish bankers and the immigrants were the root of all political evil, did he completely believe in the leader. He admitted that he did not really identify himself with the leader but *acted* this identification, performed his own enthusiasm, and thus participated in the leader's performance. It is through this performance that Jack managed to strike a balance between his continuous desire for love and protection and his realization that something was not quite right with his sudden devotion to this leader and the group. And it was probably the suspicion of this fictitiousness that made him stay in therapy so as to figure out what was happening to him. However, once he recognized the 'phoniness' of his identification with the leader, he also realized the extent to which his inability to come to terms with his father's (and his own) 'weakness' made him susceptible to this type of identification. This also made him aware of how recent social changes which had systematically contributed to the disintegration of the role of the father could potentially increase men's enthusiastic identifications with God-like leaders (i.e., primal fathers) and intensify the destructive dynamics of their groups.

Conclusion

The above case study illustrates the potential for critical engagement with the existing social conditions that characterizes the Freudian emphasis on the importance of the role of the (primal) father. But can we locate the same potential in the Lacanian approach? Following Freud, Lacanians argue that beneath the surface of social and political turmoil that is characteristic of the modern world there is a significant problem that remains unrecognized: the problem of the father. It is the problem to which Nietzsche enigmatically pointed in his devastating diagnosis of the modern predicament: *God is dead*. The result of this underlying crisis is that the contemporary social and political world both passionately desires the death of traditional patriarchal authority and seeks to resurrect it. As the renowned Lacanian, Richard Boothby (2005), puts it:

> The overall picture, if we size things up from a global point of view, is thus a decidedly mixed one. ... Modernity is itself precisely this mixture of opposites. We thus arrive at this paradoxical conclusion: the contemporary world is *both less and more patriarchal than ever before.*
>
> (p. 195)

As we have already mentioned above, the Lacanian solution to this simultaneous decrease and increase of the power of patriarchy is to abstract the authority of the father from its concrete socio-historical basis and transform it into a transcendent symbolic function (i.e., the Law of the – dead primal – Father). By assigning a transcendental locus to patriarchy, it preserves its status as it remains unaffected by historical changes and appropriations which either increase or decrease its power. In other words, the Lacanian account converts the current socio-historical absence of a concrete paternal authority into a universal, ahistorical, phantom-like patriarchal structure which is so alien and external to men that they cannot either interact with it or identify it directly with that which goes on within their esteemed inner life.

In contrast, the Freudian account, in its insistence on the importance and continued relevance of certain concrete paternal qualities which have become outdated in the present, provides men with the opportunity to critically engage with their fathers' 'weaknesses' and preserve aspects of their personality which are still individually and socially useful so as to challenge the insidious power of the various phantom-like patriarchal structures which generate violence and alienation. In this sense, Freudian theory invokes not only a past notion of fatherhood which is obsolete but also a future one that needs to be recaptured and reconstructed.

6

On Men's Friendships with Other Men

Larry O'Carroll

If the socially instituted is to be reproduced as an ongoing culture, as a living form of life, human subjects must unconsciously exercise psychic capacities, including defences of the ego. For that reason alone, it is problematical to assume that the existing specificities of historical times simply 'get inside' human material. No instance of the psyche can be conceived ever to have acted and desired in punctual accord with the instituted life sanctioned by the social domain (this argument is developed more extensively in my paper 'Achieving Our Country: Ethnic Difference and White Man's Racism', Chapter 9 in this book). For the purposes of this chapter, therefore, focusing on an affectional bond such as a man's friendship with another man obliges us to look 'beneath' the historico-cultural appearances if we are to understand the processes responsible for furnishing its psychic conditions of existence.

It is true, of course, that diverse forms of *philia* (the terms 'friendship', 'male friendship' and *'philia'* will be used interchangeably throughout the chapter) have been instituted and celebrated in the 'West'. And we have only to think of the educational-cum-erotic case of the ancient Greek world (Foucault, 1986), the friendships between monks in the early Christian monastic tradition (Foucault, 1990), or, coming up to date, the delight male friends can now take in accompanying each other to the cinema, pub or football match to appreciate that forms of friendship are as much socially instituted practices as psychically conditioned affairs of the heart. That taken for granted, the important consideration is that many accounts of friendship, albeit problematical accounts, could be constructed by reading between the lines of the multiple modes of psychoanalytic theory available to us today. Yet, to whom are we to turn, for friendship's sake – to Freud, Klein, Winnicott, Kohut, to which Lacan's 'return to Freud' could be added?

Two additional considerations will hopefully help to orient the reader. First, since what follows will be misunderstood if read as proffering even the rudiments of a psychoanalytically informed, global theory of *philia*, it will be best approached as a series of fragmentary writings (see Flax, 1991). To pursue that aim, a critical stance toward how Freud and Klein conceived of 'sublimation' and 'psychic representation' has been adopted, and the writing of Laplanche (1987, 1999a, 1999e) used to reflect on whether psychoanalysis can overcome its marginalization of friendship. Secondly, some of the men with whom I have worked therapeutically, sometimes over several years, have had an instrumental, 'what's-in-it-for-me?' attitude to what it is to be the friend of another man. Although there has been much animated talk of enjoying many an occasion together, and of sharing some interests, such men, it could be thought, have unwittingly furnished evidence for the claim that all men are 'emotionally illiterate'. That humiliating proposal will be dismissed here, by use of Laplanche's post-Lacanian return to Freud. Of particular interest will be whether the narcissistic ego, born in protest against the Other, sexuality, can be conceived to furnish the foundation of *philia* (see Gaitanidis (2007) for a wide-ranging collection of essays on the concept(s) of narcissism in contemporary psychoanalytic thought).

'Excellence' and generosity

Let us set aside how socially instituted ways of belief, conduct and aspiration shape patterns of friendship so as to conduct a thought experiment. Our experiment obtains its ideal standard from Aristotle, who, following Plato in reflecting on *philia* (unsurprisingly, he was thinking of male friendships only), suggested in his *Nicomachean Ethics* (1962) that beneficence, defined by the Shorter Oxford Dictionary as 'doing good, active kindness', is the means by which the friend promotes all that is excellent in the other; all in keeping with the kind of man he could one day become. This ancient conception remains of value today, not least because it implicitly challenges the psychoanalytic focus on the past: for Aristotle, *philia* is primarily concerned with the future of our friend, not with the past or how it has shaped his current fashioning (see Nehemas, 1985).

Nevertheless, the Aristotelian *telos* of friendship chimes with a psychoanalytic thesis, one expressible by recourse to Kleinian theory. Because a whole-object bond can only exist when depressive functioning has been accessed, the 'primitive' splitting, idealization and projection mobilized to preserve the persecuted infantile ego must have been overcome, to the extent possible, and something akin to the reparative impulse have come to life if the beneficence intrinsic to friendship is to thrive (Klein 1927, 1933, 1937). Accordingly, the reciprocal generosity of friends would, on the Kleinian account of reparation, be a hard-won achievement, one which, like everything else seeded by the depressive struggle, is never finally won. In any case, and as its quotidian phenomenology suggests, *philia* has probably always been (and will remain) a work-in-process, a 'project' never finally accomplished, an ideal upon the basis of which we judge our conduct vis-à-vis our friend, and *vice versa*.

However, locating beneficence/generosity at the heart of friendship also advises that recourse to the death-trinity of destructiveness, hostility and envy, the trio of impulses which, for Kleinian thought, is launched into post-uterine life by unconscious phantasy, should be eschewed (See Hinshelwood, 1989). As Aristotle's standard of excellence bears on a man's capacity and willingness to be beneficent to his friend for the latter's sake, friendship's primary psychic condition would poorly be conceived as owing its possibility to reparative impulses built atop infantile hostility to the primary (part-) object. It is certain too, with Laplanche for company, that although friendship may find one of its psychic conditions in early care – in Winnicottian diction, in concern for the other (Winnicott, 1990) – such care must not be conceived as springing from maternal attunement alone (that Laplanche (1999c) has repudiated the Freudian concept of primal phantasy and the Kleinian concept of unconscious phantasy because of their Ptolemaism advises that Winnicott's emphasis on maternal care is unacceptable too if we are to go astray with Freud. See the last section of this chapter for a more detailed discussion of Laplanche's argument). The general point at issue here is that attempting to isolate the 'origin' of friendship in the infant's relations to the breast and the phantasy of the combined parent figure, in phantasies of the primal scene or in good enough maternal attunement will not advance our understanding of *philia*. Such accounts fall foul of Laplanche's critique of the Ptolemaism of Freudian and post-Freudian thought, and collapse two terms of Aristotelian provenance – namely, the difference between necessary and sufficient causes. That some X (say, maternal care or relatively early imaginings vis-à-vis the primal scene) furnishes the condition of some Y's later appearance does not mean that the former is the 'sufficient cause' of the latter. And albeit that X may be a 'necessary cause' of Y, of *philia* in our case, Y could in principle owe its character to psychic processes appearing well after the period of infancy and early childhood. Hence focusing on the avowed early and necessary causes of friendship in infantile experience will not meet the joyful and testing exercise of the mature self informing Aristotle's future-directed portrait of friendship.

Now, we may find it counter-intuitive to think of friendship-love and the duty of beneficence as two sides of the same affective coin, especially as we have come to believe, and to some large extent conduct ourselves, as if our desire for 'intimacy' exhausted the character of *philia* (see Giddens 1991; Rose, 1998) (the notion of 'intimacy' and with it, that of 'relationship', will, as Phillips (2000a) has implied, require thoroughgoing critique if Laplanche's version of the return to Freud is ever to command allegiance among today's psychoanalytic community. By the same token, that the focus on intimacy by Giddens (1991) and, in Foucauldian fashion, by Rose (1998) is currently sociologically and historically acceptable suggests how far-ranging the incommensurability of psychoanalysis and other forms of late-modern inquiry can go). When, however, we are prepared to acknowledge what self-testing work friendship sometimes is, the counter-intuition largely disappears. It *is* my duty, one I can choose to meet or not, to do all I can to support my friend as he strives to become a better man than he is; perhaps, a more courageous man than he has managed to be thus far; a husband more thoughtful vis-à-vis his wife; perhaps a kinder father to his children too, and more generous to himself when, as will inevitably occur, he will fail, as I shall do, to act in accord with Aristotle's ideal. Conversely, when a (putative) friendship is experienced in hyper-individualistic, unilaterally ego-serving mode and the devotion it requires has unconsciously been modelled on the love we have received or not as infants and children from our parents, we most likely have a case of illusion, in Freud's sense of the term (Freud, 1927). The man who experiences his friendship so is not 'wrong', epistemologically and ethically speaking; rather, because his friendship-experience has sprung from wholly unconscious sources in him, repetition and transference most likely govern his relations to the man he believes to be his friend.

An odd circumstance regarding the history of psychoanalysis may now be noted. In regard to friendship, the concern for the other, a concern possibly owing its basis to the good enough early care of the infant's vulnerability and omnipotence, has not received the attention it merits from psychoanalytic thought. True, there are scattered remarks in Freud's and others' writings bearing on the possibility of 'true' friendship, but they are couched in such a way that *philia* is granted little or no particularity as a love distinct from parental love, sibling love, and mature erotic love. To cite but one telling example: apropos his friendship with Wilhelm Fleiss, Freud wrote of an unruly homosexual impulse in himself as bearing responsibility for the breakdown of their relations. Of interest are possibilities the founding psycho-archaeologist, he who constructed psychoanalysis as the complex narrative of infantile sexuality, Oedipus and castration, did not – or, perhaps, refused to – entertain. As Freud reported the matter, his concern was neither the excellence of his friend nor the challenge of being generous to him under what undoubtedly were emotionally testing conditions for both of them. No, as if to furnish case-specific evidence for what had become his theory of psychical subjectivity, Freud contented himself with the ret-rospective self-analysis that a component instinct of infantile sexuality, one presumably testifying to the return of the repressed, had made amicable negotiation impossible. In opting for that 'explanation', how-ever, Freud oddly acquitted himself of fault, given what was already becoming his emphasis on intentional unconscious mental activity.

For all of us interested in psychoanalysis, let alone for those who practice in the tradition of therapeutic engagement invented by Freud, it is dismaying, somewhat ironic too, that he did not inquire of him-self: do I want this friendship to continue? Have I lost faith in Fleiss? If I have, what does that say of the kind of man I am, and he is? Were we ever friends at all? To the contrary, Freud was ruthless, probably in the service of his conquistador's ambition to be like Copernicus and Darwin in wounding our species' narcissism, and in the light of his dawning appreciation that most of Fleiss's theories were crazy. His self-analysis, therefore, that unique exercise of the self never to be repeated, so Jones (1980) and Anzieu (1986) among other of his biographers have claimed, functioned to prevent him from considering his supposed friend in other than an objectivizing manner. Freud used Fleiss as an 'it', for as long as he proved useful to him, only to discard him when his utility had been exhausted (see Jacoby, 1984; Spence, 1994).

To the objection that saying so is to be 'judgmental', it is not my inten-tion, if only not to fall foul of the pot-and-kettle principle, to excoriate Freud for his abandonment of Fleiss. The point worth making here is that were we ever to have a general theory of *philia*, even a theory for which the excellence of the other were the primary driver and unruly homosexual impulses could become wholly conscious, it would not say anything worthwhile of whether it is good to live, as best any man can, what it is to be a friend. On this view of the matter, psychoanalysis does not need a theory of *philia*, since a friendship thrives, not because it is or could ever be superintended by *sophia* (wisdom), which Aristotle associated with the pursuit of scientific knowledge; no, the conduct of a friendship may rely on *phronesis*, the term he used to describe everyday practical activities capable of enhancing the quality of life (Aristotle, 1962).

Because it is the excellence of the other which, on the Aristotelian portrayal of *philia*, exercises friends, the argument thus far has been that a whole-object psychic economy supplies one of its necessary conditions. Furthermore, if the potential excellence of his friend is to motivate a man, both men must exercise beneficence – a requirement presupposing that the other has become a fellow human subject with a life and mind of his own. Thus omnipotent projection, idealization and other defensive processes Klein (1946) held to be characteristic of infancy must have been sufficiently mitigated to allow self and other to be experienced as autonomous subjects – a condition requiring the friends' capacity for post-transference relations, hence an ego capable of containing pre-Oedipal and Oedipal unconscious anxieties. Perhaps that is why no psychoanalytic literature exists on male friendship *per se*; it is as if its clinical focus on the obstacles to human association has functioned to silence Freud's and his followers' curiosity apropos a realm of experience of profound importance to many of us for fashioning a satisfying, enriching life.

To be sure, friendship cannot protect us from life's losses and sometimes near-devastating contingencies. But that is neither to say that it is ineffective as a source of consolation in times of woe nor that psychoanalysis has been wise to overlook its *differentia specifica*. Additionally, inasmuch as a friendship may be said to rely on the existence of the 'I' and 'Thou', in other words on what, for want of a better term, we may call a strong ego, the suspicion is warranted that focusing on unconscious mental activity alone will ill-serve our understanding. Is not conscious reflection devoted to the needs of one's friend, as well as examination of one's conduct vis-à-vis him, virtues without which a friendship cannot be sustained? If so, there is a strong case for arguing that contemporary psychoanalytic theory is obliged to re-envision the ego as more than some abstracted reality-tester – a proposal which, far from supporting Lacan's metapsychological reformulation of the ego as the seat of psychic misrecognition – by extension, his linguistification of desire – requires their unequivocal rejection (Lacan, 1937; Castoriadis, 1984, 1987; Whitebook, 1995).

Sublimation and psychic representation

Could sublimation be the principal psychic capacity required for *philia* to prosper? Yes and no will be our answer, as much depends on how the process is conceived. Laplanche and Pontalis (1983) define sublimation as a

> process postulated by Freud to account for human activities which have no apparent connection with sexuality but which are assumed to be motivated by the force of the sexual instinct. The main types of activity described by Freud as sublimated are artistic creation and intellectual inquiry. The instinct is said to be sublimated in so far as it is diverted towards a new, non-sexual aim and in so far as its objects are socially useful ends.
>
> (p. 431)

For Freud, sublimation was intimately related to the sexual 'instincts' inasmuch as its mechanism functioned to divert the aim of sexual satisfaction towards a non-sexual aim, 'to which a particular society assigns great value' (ibid., p. 432). In this view, friendship *must* qualify as a sublimated activity since, on Freud's assumptions, its possibility, unconscious root and exercise rely on redirecting the aim of infantile autoerotic pleasure. In addition, because for Freud (1905) the infant and young child, whose 'component instincts' await organization by Oedipus and castration, is incapable of sublimation, sublimatory activity must be a late-appearing capacity. And when libido 'places extraordinarily large amounts of force at the disposal of civilised activity, and [does so] in virtue of its especially marked characteristic of being able to displace its aim without materially diminishing its intensity', plainly Freud required the category of sublimation if his insistence that infantile sexuality lay at the root of all varieties of human pleasure was to prove coherent (ibid., p. 187).

Freud had hoped to include an essay on sublimation, so Jones (1980) informs us, in his *Papers on Metapsychology* (Freud, 1915). Why did he not do so? A theoretical imperative faced him: he *had* to conceive of sublimation as other than a defensive process because, in the terms introduced by his structural model, he understood a defence bearing on a component instinct as serving to forbid the expression of an ego-dystonic id-derivative (Freud, 1923). The ego unconsciously mobilizes a defence to protect the organism from incursion by some facet of the unconscious repressed. If, then, sublimation was to be conceived as replacing a once-sexual aim by a desexualized socially valued end, and if the very notion of sublimation evoked for Freud the chemical process whereby 'a body is caused to pass directly from a solid to a gaseous state' (Laplanche and Pontalis, ibid., p. 432), surely it would have been more helpful, more accurate too, to write of the *transformation* effected by sublimation than of its mechanism as the 'displacement' of a formerly sexual aim. Whereas displacement summons thought of the 'original' aim subsequently appearing under another guise, 'transformation' suggests that the original phenomenon, ruled by the pleasure principle, has succumbed to some sort of process of translation (see Phillips, 2000b). Much the same may be said of 'substitute formation': because the substitute designates 'symptoms – or equivalent formations such as parapraxis, jokes, etc. – in so far as they *stand for* [*re*-present] unconscious contents', logically speaking sublimation and substitution must be different psychic processes (Laplanche and Pontalis, 1983, p. 434; emphasis added).

The concept of 'psychic(al) representation' is at issue, here – that is to say, how, for psychoanalysis, the once psychically infantile comes to be represented by another, more encultured and mature activity, in the experience of the subject. As Hirst (1979) has argued of the recourse to the category of representation in Marxist analysis, however, if all so-called representation could do is manifest or re-express that which it avowedly *re*-presents, the vehicle or means of representation (modern mass media, in the case of Marxist theory) is being accorded no effectivity in its own right. The photograph, the news report, the newspaper editorial, the situation comedy would all function as mere stand-ins, as ciphers, for the structure of class relations theorized as characterizing all capitalist economies. Hence Hirst's conclusion: the category of representation, as deployed in the Marxist discourse of his time, required radical re-elaboration in such a way that the means of representation would be granted a 'making-difference' effectivity, for which purpose he urged the replacement of representation by 'signification' (ibid.).

The purchase of Hirst's critique for psychoanalytic thought is that if all later psychic representation could achieve were to function as a stand-in for some earlier-occurring state(s), our talk of the psyche as accessing reality-testing, depressive functioning, concern for the other, and so on, would be vacuous. After all, would not my devotion to my friend (rather, what I self-servingly call my 'devotion' to him) be just another case, one among the billions, of a grown-up infant's denial, or search for sexual pleasure, or transference? With that question to the fore, it is clear that if psychoanalysis is to continue to use the notion of 'psychic representation', the means of representation must be granted effectivity so as to avoid reduction to the origin – to infancy.

It is true too that the activities to be counted as sublimated are 'badly demarcated' in Freud's *oeuvre* (Laplanche and Pontalis, 1983, p. 431). Is other than intellectual work to count; does parental sacrifice count, though it could be 'narcissistic' at heart, always and everywhere (Freud,

1914); what of a teacher's devotion to her students, regardless of time and place; and when historical and anthropological differences count, what are we to make of the fact that the 'sublimated' cannot be separated from the locally instituted? Whatever our answers to such questions may turn out to be, insofar as sublimation for Freud owed its possibility to a transformational process whose mechanism remained mysterious to him, our conclusion must be that he could not have accounted for *philia* when conceived as motivated by beneficence and the excellence of the other.

What of Kleinian theory, in this connection: can it account for the transformation of early object relations in such a way that the friend, no substitute or stand-in for that which has been experienced in early life, can become a loved other in his own right? It is significant in this regard that Hinshelwood (1989) does not include an entry for sublimation in *A Dictionary of Kleinian Thought*; instead, sublimation is in part discussed under the heading of 'symbol-formation', a concept owing its provenance to Klein's psychoanalyses of young children, as conducted by means of her play technique. For Klein,

> [i]n their play children represent symbolically phantasies, wishes and their experiences. Here they are employing the same language, the same archaic, phylogenetically acquired mode of expression as we are familiar with in dreams.'
>
> (Klein, cited in Hinshelwood, 1989, p. 445)

Although its concern is the symbolic character of children's play, this early text anticipates Klein's work on the vicissitudes of symbol-formation in the experience of human subjects in-the-making. And albeit that her interest was, as Hinshelwood notes, to shift from the 'the nature of the process of expression' (op.cit, p. 446) of unconscious phantasy to its contents, especially in regard to what, to the adult mind, are the extraordinarily violent phantasies infants and young children avowedly entertain of the maternal body, her early work made it possible for Segal (1950, 1957) to distinguish symbolic equation from symbolic representation. In symbolic equation the 'symbol' is experienced as the stand-in for that which it (putatively) symbolizes, hence 'attracts the same conflicts and inhibitions as the original because of the fusion of the self and the object', whereas in symbolic representation a 'true' symbol is in place, in the sense that it is 'recognized as having its own characteristics separate from that which it symbolizes' (Hinshelwood, 1989, 447–8).

Segal's distinction, it may be thought, can come to our aid as it identifies the momentous psychic difference between a friendship functioning as a stand-in for unresolved infantile anxieties and one owing its possibility to a whole-object economy. And the distinction is clinically apposite: in my experience, it has not been parental figures alone from whom angry and disappointed projections have required withdrawal; for some men presenting for what has turned out to be long-term psychodynamic engagement, the continual breakdown of their friendships has in part, I believe, been symptomatic of the 'fusion' they have unconsciously experienced between self and other. Self and other have been enmeshed to some marked degree, with the consequence that, in times of stress and trouble, everyday projections have been experienced as repeating the impingements of early life. (Such at least is how I have sought to understand such men.) If only for that reason, then, Segal's distinction has proven clinically useful: it alerts the practitioner to how psychically fragile some men can be, and to their unvoiced need to sustain friendship.

Nonetheless the distinction must be refused since, according to Laplanche (1999a), it depends, like *all* the psychoanalytic theory written since Freud's 'going astray', on a Ptolemaic recentring of the psyche. However, irrespective of the Ptolemaism of Kleinian thought, indeed of all psychoanalytic theory since Freud went astray, it is worth noting that Sandler (1988) was the first, as far as I know, to advise that we need not subscribe to the Kleinian (somewhat Gothic) portrait of the infant's struggles with persecutory anxiety to find the concepts of splitting, projective identification, and so forth, of singular clinical value.

Going astray

Let us now turn to the re-elaboration of Freudian thought undertaken by Laplanche. Of primary concern is whether what we might call his post-Lacanian return to Freud repeats the marginalization of friendship in psychoanalytic thought, a question we will consider by focusing on the concepts of primal seduction, the ego, narcissism, and the Oedipus complex.

It was Freud who first linked the birth of the ego with narcissism by recourse to the notion of 'a new psychical action':

> [W]e are bound to suppose that a unity comparable to the ego cannot exist in the individual from the start; the ego has to be developed. The auto-erotic instincts [*sic*], however, are there from the very first; so

there must be something added to auto-erotism – a new psychical action – in order to bring about narcissism.

(Freud 1914, p. 77)

Following on from the auto-eroticism of infancy, 'a new psychical action' must occur if the ego is to appear and, if later, the tripartite psyche comprising id, ego and superego is to be fashioned. In conceiving the matter so, Freud was relying on two of his cardinal assumptions: 'the auto-erotic instincts' [*sic*] are 'there from the first' – a thesis depending on picturing the *infans* as at first a self-enclosed monad capable of auto-erotic pleasure; and those instincts (precisely, drives) will, upon the birth of the ego, enter into dynamic conflict with the human organism's self-preservation, for which the ego will become the vehicle of expression (Freud, 1918, 1923). There is a sizeable conceptual problem here, however, according to Laplanche, one not so much to do with how Freud conceived of 'primary' and 'secondary' narcissism (Freud, 1914) although that is of concern to him, but with the circumstance that Freud's portrayal of the psyche depends on recentring it in Ptolemaic fashion. As I have put it elsewhere:

What Laplanche calls Freud's 'going astray', a disastrous shift from a Copernican to a Ptolemaic conception of the psyche, is ... at stake here ... [F]or Laplanche, the going astray occurred when Freud replaced his early seduction theory, for which sexuality was a 'foreign body' breaking in from a source external to the infant, by a conception focusing on, amongst other matters, the primal fantasies later held to organise the 'component instincts' of infantile sexuality (Freud 1895, 1905). Moreover, Freud's suppression of sexuality as an 'alien-ness' decentring the psyche led him to a Ptolemaic theory of subjectivity. The analogy is with Ptolemy, for whom the sun and planets revolved around the earth, whereas Freud's principal discovery, that sexuality is radically Other, an implanted alterity vis-à-vis the ego, constitutes the Copernican point of departure for a licit psychoanalytic understanding of subjectivity.

(O'Carroll, in Gaitanidis with Curk, 2007, p. 94)

When Laplanche's thesis that sexuality is implanted in the *infans* by unconscious maternal activity is accepted, the psycho-developmental meaning of narcissism is transformed. Since, from the first, the infant has been in receipt of the enigmatic sexual significations of the maternal unconscious, the appearance of narcissism constitutes a closing-down to primal seduction. That is to say, because the mother cannot help but libidinally cathect her breast in the service of feeding her infant (her breasts have already been eroticized by her, her partner, and the culture at large), it is the constellation of enigmatic significations she sends her infant's way which is repudiated when narcissism and, with it, the ego, are born. Laplanche's reformulation of psychoanalytic theory thereby reverses the direction of libidinal cathexis we find in usual Ptolemaic psychoanalytic thought. The consequence is that the infant's 'pre'-sexualization by maternal care, his primal seduction, propels him into a human world characterized by *der Andere* and *das Andere*. *Der Andere* is the object, at first the mother, whose enigmatic messages render the infant a stranger-to-himself when his ego closes him down. And *das Andere* is 'the thing', the alien, seductive sexuality upon the repudiation of which is founded the infant's 'I' (Laplanche 1999c, pp. 135–6). In short, the sexuality of the (m)other, testifying to an already sexualized world, is the alien-stranger setting psychic differentiation in train.

This noted, what is the pertinence of Laplanche's reconfiguration of Freudian theory for the Aristotelian portrayal of friendship? Two points are worth making, in reply, the first of which directly bears on the talk we hear nowadays of the 'emotional illiteracy' of men – of all men without exception, it seems. Apart from the vulgar, biologistic conception of gender on which such talk depends (does not 'emotional (il)literacy' reduce to an expression of an always already sexed subject?), what pot is it which calls the kettle black, there? Projection, given the thesis of primal seduction, could provide the key. Thinking of all men as being emotionally illiterate fails to recognize that it is 'miraculous' how any human being, given our primal seduction and repudiation of the (m)other, could ever be otherwise, let alone sustain any 'relationship' at all (Phillips, 2000a). Accordingly, speaking of men and women as near-different classes in regard to the affective states of which humankind is capable is to forget that, regardless of the infant's sex, the emergence of the ego and its narcissism relies on repudiating the maternal libidiniza-tion of the infant's body.

Preposterous talk of men's emotional illiteracy, moreover, is, from the Laplanchean perspective, on all fours with those psychoanalytic theories which, in their different ways, foreground maternal attunement as the condition *par excellence* of what will later become psychical subjectivity – for example, Stern (1985) and Winnicott (1965). In other words, that Laplanche writes of the *implantation* of sexuality, of a *seduc-tion* decentring the proto-psychical subject, tells us, in a manner chiming with Freud's conviction that sexuality endlessly troubles humankind, that an inassimilable Big Other, sexuality, is every infant's Copernican fate irrespective of what will later become a socially engendered identity (see Freud, 1930).

The second point concerns the place of the Oedipus complex in Laplanchean thought. Suppose that a man's devotion to his friend owes its foundation, its 'necessary cause', to the first protest issued to a human world impregnated with sexual significations. Imagine too that it is the ego's initial narcissistic closure which seeds what will come much later in the infant's experience – the possibility of friendship. Were such things to be so, it would be difficult to resist the conclusion that Freud's concept of the Oedipus complex mistook a 'cause' for an 'effect'. It is not via the Oedipus (and, in tandem with it, castration) that the boy is launched into the extra-familial world. His primal repudiation, somehow simultaneously constitutive of the ego and carried by its protest, performs the primary humanizing task. *That* was what Freud and all subsequent Ptolemaic psychoanalytic discourse repressed when he 'abandoned' his early seduction theory, only to erect a Ptolemaic conception of the primal phantasies in its stead (Laplanche, 1999a, 1999d).

Conclusion

Are we to conclude that Laplanche has abandoned the centrality Freud accorded the Oedipus complex? Certainly, we can read him as already having done so. Laplanche renders primal seduction a perversion of maternal care and locates psychic structuration as beginning with a novel body ego – the auto-prohibiting, protesting infant – responsible for the first repression and primal closure. But whether we read Laplanche so is not the major consideration, for a concept is still missing – the concept of the structure or series of psychic mechanisms which, in lieu of the Oedipus, would fashion the 'difference' between mature hetero- and homosexual love, on the one hand, and *philia*, on the other. That is to say, what happens after the initial, humanizing closing down such that friendship can become a desexualized, sublimatory practice remains to be conceived.

We appreciate now why much theoretical re-elaboration remains to be done by a psychoanalyst hyper-critical of Freud if the psychoanalysts and psychoanalytic psychotherapists of the future are to hear men's suffering vis-à-vis friendship anew. Saying so brings me, finally, to an historical fact of our time. Since it is impossible to believe that going-astray practitioners have disrespected the friendships of their male clients, we may wonder how it is that what has escaped current clinical theory has nonetheless proven therapeutic by way of supporting men to be better friends. Given the suspicion that the Laplanchean return will not come to friendship's aid, perhaps the best to be done is allow a Ptolemaic psychoanalyst, Winnicott, to advise us. Leave paradox alone, resist being clever, and allow the other to speak the excellent interpretations.

7
Deconstructing the Homosexual–Heterosexual Divide

Larry O'Carroll

In the early 1980s Kenneth Plummer (1981) co-edited a volume of essays informed by, among other currents of thought, the sociology of deviance and the writings of Michel Foucault. By focusing on the making of a sexual 'type', the contributors to the volume presented a plausible case for viewing what nowadays we call the male homosexual as an identity-marker invented by what Foucault (1981) had termed the historical apparatus of sexuality (for Foucault, an 'apparatus' is to be understood as an assemblage of knowledges (note the plural) and practices (together, they constitute 'discourses') that can be analysed as having had systematic effects on how we live today). And, in doing so, they advised of how we should approach the homoeroticism of ancient Greece and imperial Rome: since 'homosexuality' as a working social category has been fashioned in recent historical time, care needs to be taken in attempting to understand figures like Alexander, Hephastion, and Mark Anthony. Although these figures experienced the male body as erotic, it would be grossly anachronistic to claim that such men were 'homosexual', or, for that matter, 'bisexual', in the modern meaning of these terms. For a multifaceted history has intervened, one so complex that it is dizzying to imagine how they could have engaged in same-sex practices without it dawning on them that thereby they were expressing anything approaching an 'abnormal' manner of wedding what we nowadays call 'personality' to sexual conduct. Doubtless, the homosexual as a 'veritable species', to use Foucault's description, is a creation of modernity.

Now, in taking this historical novelty on board we could easily conclude that a great deal must be awry with psychoanalytic theory. After all, ever since Freud psychoanalysis has deployed historical developments to construct its categories of sense. An example of which Foucault

(1981) has written immediately springs to mind – the 'moral panic' over children's masturbation in the nineteenth century. Utilizing that panic in his inimitable style, Freud used an 'event' for the purpose of representing masturbation as definitive of the auto-eroticism of the infant, always and everywhere. Thereby, a historically specific occurrence – so Foucault, genealogist of sexuality, thinks of the matter – was universalized by Freud in the form of a species-wide organ-pleasure awaiting organization by the Oedipus complex. From this and similar instances it could be concluded that Freud's willingness to universalize the historically emergent unintentionally witnessed how the articulation of any vision of the psyche must draw on what is available in the culture of the time. Going further, the conclusion might be that, because it is apt to (psycho-) ontologize the historically particular, it is about time that a therapeutic method fashioned on the basis of a compound of conceptual dexterity and unacknowledged theft were pensioned-off.

We should resist such a hasty conclusion, not least because adoption of an illusory God's-eye perspective is required if we are to hold that Freud was mistaken in making of childhood masturbation what he did. For the time being, suffice it to note that although the universalizing ambition of psychoanalysis will be defended here, how it has understood male same-sex desire, that is to say, male homosexuality, will be critically examined (where appropriate, I will be using the term 'male same-sex desire' (or 'same-sex desire') rather than 'homosexuality', since the latter term comes replete with reproductivist, bad-Darwinian, baggage). It is true that matters have begun to change over the last 20 years or so – for example, in the writings of Kenneth Lewes (1989) and Robert Stoller (1975), among a few others. The gay man is not impeached for his 'abnormality' there. Nevertheless, it is fair to conclude that Freud's heirs – and with licence from the founder of psychoanalysis, we will see – have continued to collude with the oppression visited upon men-loving men by a late-modern 'western' culture yet to come to terms with its debts to Judeo-Christian prejudice (Boswell, 1980). However, because any such critical engagement must respect the psycho-symbolic kind of sense-making Freud created, it will be argued that psychoanalysis is neither ahistorical nor essentialist, in the usual acceptation of the terms. Supposing otherwise always leads to the sociologization of Freud's achievement, hence to the expulsion of the agency of the psychic unconscious.

In the second section of the chapter we will encounter why it is necessary to retain the distinction Freud drew between the aim and object of the human sexual drive in *Three Essays on the Theory of Sexuality* (Freud

1905, hereafter *The Essays*). It is on that basis alone that male same-sex desire will be appreciated for what it is – as a universal possibility, an unremarkable 'preference', as just one way among others of becoming a sexual being who, to some getting-on degree, has left the incestuous relations of childhood behind. But, an important qualification is necessary. In his attempt to distinguish the aim from the object, Freud insisted that same-sex desire is the consequence of an arrest in (psychical) development. In other words, he embraced contradictory visions of human sexuality. One way of picturing the human sexual drive is to envision it as a force for which being 'heterosexual' or 'homosexual' is an irrelevance. Yet the promulgator of this vision hesitates, draws back, as if horrified at his own audacity, to insist that the drive's proper destiny is 'the primacy of the genitals; in another diction, the 'Multiply Your Kind' of biblical provenance. Despite his expressed intention, therefore, we must note that Freud unintentionally licensed the homophobic orthodoxy of the psychoanalytical writing following him by conceiving of same-sex desire. An example of that orthodoxy is furnished by Melanie Klein's thought, while the work of Stoller has valorized and broadened Freud's distinction between the aim and object.

So far my concern has been with psychoanalysis – with its discursive particularity and how it has pictured same-sex desire. As its title suggests however, the chapter has another aim. In asking, 'will heterosexuals and homosexuals always exist?' I am looking forward, much like Judith Butler (1993, 2004) and Nancy Chodorow (1994), to a community in which our obsession with the erotic object – with what sex does what to whom, and with what part of the body – will long have passed away. Due in part to the dissemination of the notion of 'compromise formation', it will be a culture in which speaking of hetero- and homosexuals will have become the kind of talk capable of eliciting condescending comments from most of our descendants. Yet against the hope for the good tomorrow must be juxtaposed what gay men's political action has achieved in recent years. Because what they have won by way of respect for, and tolerance of sexual preference remains, and in all likelihood will remain a contested victory, we would be foolish to believe that we have no need of our erotic identities anymore. After all, historical creations can stick, make progress worth having possible, albeit that they can disappoint our hope for the punctual arrival of the good tomorrow.

The third section of the chapter will return to 'history' – to the two, radically dissimilar ways of conceiving of systematic (psycho-) historical effects as represented by the genealogical and psychoanalytical modes of inquiry. Can they come to our aid by informing a sexual politics of use to our children and their descendants? Genealogy can do so – but only once we question the oddly voluntaristic consciousness to which it can give rise. In this regard, Foucault's later writing on governmentality, when combined with his post-Marxist vision of the local intellectual deflates all naïve hope for the appearance of a better order of things. Psychoanalysis has some useful things to say to sexual politics, too. Irrespective of how some feminist theory has sought to mine its conceptual resources for the purpose of exploding the effects of patriarchy, one way of reading psychoanalysis is to encounter it as simply advising that, for the foreseeable future, political action will have no choice but to retain much of the vision of the erotic bequeathed to us.

Putting it so identifies the main concern of the chapter. We have two useful perspectives available for thinking about the community of the future; a future in which some human creatures with a penis will not be calumnied for wedding their search for erotic love to bodies like their own. The one, the genealogy of sexuality, understands psychoanalysis as among the discourses in our midst that have penned their accounts of subjectivity by ignoring what the history of social relations has made us. There is much to be said in defence of that perspective. On the other hand, psychoanalysis is a mode of inquiry whose indefatigable suspicion shows us, if only we could realize it, that heterosexuality and male homosexuality are psychical twins. In other words, although Foucault, Freud, and their descendants are destined to pass each other by, their incommensurable accounts of our condition are good-to-believe.

History and essence

That Freud conceives of the Oedipus complex as the gateway to humanization, as both the obstacle yet essential condition of becoming a human subject, means that the history of concern to him is that of all humans' formation as psychical subjects. The history we carry within us as the record of the always costly, irremediably traumatic, advent to fellowship is Freud's principal object of inquiry. That is to say, his thought is concerned with the existence and effects of a symbolic, psychical domain interpenetrating all historical societies; of a domain irreducible to, as the anthropologist conceives of them, the practices, customs and webs of belief responsible for fashioning specific modes or forms of subjectivity (Hirst and Woolley, 1982). Moreover, this universally extant psychical domain owes its instantiation in all human subjects to the linked processes of anaclisis ('propping') on the vital functions, and to primal fantasy. It is by these means, according to Freud, that what were once the components of a polymorphously perverse infantile sexuality assume the organization upon which all sociality depends. The details of the argument do not matter at this point. What is important is that, for Freud, all sociality, hence the very possibility of all transformations wrought in historical time, depend upon the post-Oedipal reconfiguration of a primary psychic 'chaos' characterized at first by infantile auto-eroticism, and later by incestuous desire.

Freud can be no modern human scientist, therefore. His writing does not focus on the different 'personalities', self-representations and practices produced by historical time and cultural location. Beneath the surface of dissimilarity, the one psyche is ever present, a psyche whose capacities no culture can create. We have only to think of the defensive processes of repression, projection, idealization and identification to appreciate that the psyche of which Freud writes exercises capacities upon which all historical times and cultural *milieux* depend. In this sense, Freud elaborates a theory that conflicts with so much that our modern human sciences advise. Inasmuch as he understands the psychical domain as pertaining to the construction of all human subjects, it is the organization of psychical relations as the condition of association which matters to him, not what place and time occasion by way of practice, belief, and self-representation.

Yet, the appearances notwithstanding, Freud is not being ahistorical in conceiving things so. Rather, he invents another kind of history – the history for which there cannot exist a consciousness of passing time, of the transience of all attachment and achievement, let alone our aware-ness of the existence of others, without there being oedipalized psyches prepared to mourn. When we forget this, or insist on smuggling in some other way of accounting which Freudian suspicion contests, we are often in the business of valorizing what Wilfrid Sellars christened as *The Myth of the Given*.

Although Sellars (1967) was concerned with empiricist philosophy, what he has to say is useful for our purposes. Roughly speaking, when we are wedded to the Myth of the Given, we think that as all things in The World Out There exist 'independently' of us, all that needs to be done is register how all given things impact on Mind. From that bad, if prestigious, idea has sprung the conclusion that it is the task of inquiry – of all inquiry, irrespective of the objects of sense being considered – to 'correspond to' what is given, since knowledge consists in 'representing' the given to Mind. Not the least problem with this, from the psychoanalytical point of view, is that the 'mind' required by empiricist myth can be no internally differentiated psyche. Nor can it belong to a creature, the human being, whose first principle of operation will forever remain wish fulfillment.

Clearly, we do not have to endorse Freud's vision of the psyche's two principles of operation to appreciate the point at issue here (Freud, 1911). For any variant of psychoanalytical theory the psyche must be conceived as being as much an organizer of its 'sense impressions' as a human material capable of registering what will come to be experienced as the Out There for it. Hence how we conceive of this necessary organization being accomplished is not in question – for example, by receipt of good-enough mothering (Winnicott), by advent to depressive functioning (Klein), or by means of accession to the Symbolic register of existence (Lacan). The crucial consideration is that an empiricist position always puts the cart of The World Out There before the horse of a psyche capable of finding any 'out there' whatsoever of libidinal interest. That accepted, it is but a short step to thinking that since a human being's advent to social relations requires a work of psychical production and organization, accounting for the history of that being's becoming a desiring subject is not a task for any kind of usual historical writing, a genealogy included. I will return to this point in the concluding section of the chapter.

Now consider an essentialist position, the logic of which goes something like this. Some aspect of the social-historical world's furniture is always and will forever be determinative in the same way. Often enough 'nature' (qua realm of the biologically given) when set against 'culture' (qua domain of social-historical practices) has categorically operated in this manner – as have justice, femininity/masculinity, and madness, too. When social theory has recourse to such essentialist doctrine, that which lies beneath the appearance of things ('the essence') must be brought into the light of day so as to afford social theory its critical purchase upon the present. And if the essence has become 'alienated' – usually by virtue of class relations and/or patriarchy, according to usual conceptions – social theory will have at its disposal a means of engaging with our present-day fallen state. Essentialism, then, when combined with some thesis of alienation, is not only a secularized genus of the mythopoeic doctrine of Original Sin; it is a demand exerted on social theory to restore what has been lost. That is one reason why essentialism and Freudian thought have proven so incompatible, since, for Freud, part of being human is to grieve the always lost, in particular our desire to remain in the pre-Oedipal twilight of His Majesty the Baby.

Nonetheless, it can appear that Freud pens an essentialist theory because of the manner in which he links the oedipal ordering of sexuality with 'subjectifying' loss. Does Freud not hold that the one-and-same sexuality always plays the same role in social-historical relations? Will always prove asymptotic to the ego in us because the unconscious repressed will forever function in the modality of 'another scene of action'? Will always be responsible for our neurotic affections, since, at heart, neurosis testifies to a failure of the repression of incestuous desire? Yes, he does. However, as we shall shortly see, if such claims are to be taken as witnessing the adoption of an essentialist position, we may as well call any general theory of sociality 'essentialist'. That is to say, a general, universalizing claim about what it is to be human in any regime of social relations must be distinguished from an essentialist position.

Psychosexuality

How construct the required distinction? Freud's answer is to conceive of human sexuality not as a biological datum, as a given man–woman attraction, chemical or otherwise, but as a drive that must succumb to the organization necessitated by the incest taboo, the linchpin of cultural association. And, it is from that perspective that he writes that it is heterosexuality that presents the greatest explanatory problem – the test case, if we will – to psychoanalysis: not same-sex desire, paedophilia, fetishism, the cod-theatre of sadomasochism, but heterosexuality (Freud, 1905). Why is this, seemingly extraordinary, advice proffered?

No doubt Freud had in mind a number of related theses that had become fundamental for him by 1905, the publication date of *The Essays*. No pre-programmed object of pleasure exists for the sexual drive. The object must be found, discovered, instituted as the means by which erotic satisfaction will be achieved, for otherwise human sexuality, akin to a biological instinct, would be but some wired behaviour elicited by the 'appropriate' environmental stimuli, hence a plenitude involving neither lack nor loss. Moreover, sexual pleasure in adulthood, irrespective of the form it assumes, is to be conceived as always harking back to routes of excitation and discharge established in early childhood (ibid.). Far more is at stake in this proposal than lamely claiming that the past informs the present. For Freud enters another insistence: regardless of what we call sexual orientation, the powers of the psychically past, when taken in tandem with the role defence plays in the production of all human subjects, inevitably engender some measure of psychical conflict for all of us. The implication is perspicuous: that the achievement of heterogenital pleasure is a compromise formation unites it with what is another, equally difficult, psychical achievement, namely same-sex desire. As Kenneth Lewes (1989) has put it:

> It is not accurate to speak of 'normal' or 'natural' development in the case of the Oedipus Complex, since these terms suggest an orderly efflorescence of possibilities inherent in the individual before he reaches the oedipal stage. The mechanisms of the Oedipus Complex are really a series of psychic traumas, and all results of it are neurotic compromise formations. Since even optimal development is the result of trauma, the fact that a certain development results from a 'stunting' or 'blocking' or 'inhibition' of another possibility does not distinguish it from other developments. So all the results of the Oedipus Complex are traumatic, and, for similar reasons, all are 'normal'.
>
> (p. 223)

Lewes proposes a thesis that, although present in Freud's writing, was subsequently 'repressed' by him, most likely in the service of bringing his thought into elective affinity with the Darwinian evolutionary theory he so much admired. Remember that Freud decomposed the sexual drive into four elements – its pressure, source, aim, and object (Freud, 1905). Stemming from endogenous sources, the pressure sets psychical work in train, whether by action, defence, or dreaming. The drive's source lies in the erogenous zones of the body – not only in the mouth, anus, and genitals, but also, so Freud came to believe, in the eyes. Next we have the drive's aim, 'pleasure', to be understood as the satisfaction of endogenously arising excitations. At first satisfaction is sought in a disorganized manner by the infant and young child, as excitation has yet to succumb to the canalization required by the incest taboo. It will only be upon 'resolution' of the Oedipus complex, when the boy has identified with paternal prohibition, that the primacy of the genitals will transform the erotic currents of childhood. And lastly, there is the drive's object, its most universally variant feature, apropos of which Freud was to enter a note on the ancient Greeks, in one of the many additions he interpolated into the original text of *The Essays*. Whereas 'we' (in the West) privilege the object, he writes, 'they' privileged the 'instinct' – more precisely, the drive.

I will return to this note when discussing the work of Stoller. In the meantime, let us accompany Freud in his decomposition of the sexual drive. Two questions arise when we do so. What does 'the primacy of the genitals' mean? Plainly, Freud is thinking of has heterosexuality as, to his mind, it represents the 'optimal' development a psychically organized sexual impulse can attain. Yet he is clear too, interestingly enough, that 'normality' is an ideal fiction (ibid.). The second question: how can it be that, after insisting on the object's variability, Freud nevertheless declares that male same-sex desire betokens 'a certain arrest in development'? The relevant text – a letter, dated 9 April 1935, to the mother of a homosexual son – reads as follows:

> I gather from your letter that your son is a homosexual ... Homoeroticism is assuredly no advantage, but it is nothing to be ashamed of, no vice, no degradation, it cannot be classified as an illness; we consider it to be a variation of the sexual function produced by a certain arrest of development ... It is a great injustice to persecute homosexuality as a crime and a cruelty too ... If [your son] is unhappy, neurotic, torn by conflicts, inhibited in his social life, analysis may bring harmony, peace of mind, full efficiency, whether he remains a homosexual or gets changed.
>
> (Freud, cited in Sturbin, 1994, pp. 90–1)

Although he is 'homosexual', this man can be helped by psychoanalysis to experience a quotidian contentment – that 'ordinary misery' of which Freud had written earlier in his career. However, that use is made of the phrase 'arrest in development' poses a problem. How can it be that same-sex desire is 'normal' – so much so that all group endeavour is to be understood as having its conditions of existence in sublimated homoerotic desire (Freud, 1921) – simultaneously as it constitutes an arrest? The only possible answer is that Freud's developmental ideal of genital primacy designates the psychically organized position of being equipped to reproduce our kind. However, if Freud had understood the primacy of the genitals as an easily realized goal or final end, he could not have conceived of the neuroses as issuing from a *failure* of repression. By the same token, he could not have understood the 'perversions' as the 'negative of the neuroses' – 'negative' because, in his view, the perversions make use of the 'component instincts' of sexuality in a manner a neurosis is unconsciously designed to prevent (Freud, 1905). Moreover, same-sex desire – what Freud on occasion refers to as 'inversion' – is to be distinguished from *both* the perversions and the neuroses on the ground that it can be as psychically 'normal' as heterosexuality. Nevertheless, although 'genitality' cannot be understood as some unconditional goal or final end, there is still an explosive tension in Freud's thought vis-à-vis the 'normality' of same-sex desire.

Now let us ask, have we but two choices hereabouts? Must we attend to the distinction drawn between the aim and object, or abandon it? Adoption of the former option will advise that Freud's regard for Darwin's achievement is a supplement that undermines the coherence of his thought, whereas choosing the latter option will pathologize same-sex desire. However, we should note that Freud invented another means of distinguishing male same-sex desire from heterosexuality. At issue now is the difference between the 'anaclitic' and 'narcissistic' types of object-choice, one formulated on the basis of the anxieties, identifications and projections at work in all erotic love. Whereas the anaclitic type unconsciously models itself on the protection afforded the boy by the father, the narcissistic type is fuelled by the desire to find a lover who – like Leonardo, so Freud holds – will love the future homo-sexual subject as once his mother had loved him (Freud, 1910, 1914). In short, because the heterosexual man pursues a woman as Other and the homosexual an image of himself in the male Other, their choices of object issue from heterogeneous psychical histories and dynamics.

Unfortunately this second distinction, marshaled by Freud to account for *some* cases of male same-sex desire, cannot bear the theoretical weight it is designed to bear. To appreciate why, let us remember that Freud argued that as a result of the genesis of sexuality, *all* choices of object are narcissistic in origin, for upon the loss of the first object (the feeding breast), another (part-) object (the fantasmatic breast) is installed in the infant's libidinal universe. But this 'second' object, inaugurating a condition for what will later become psychical conflict, is not related to as 'part' of mother. To the contrary, on Freud's account the response of the infant to the introduction of a fantasmatic sexuality is the equally fantasmatic auto-completion known as narcissism (Freud, 1905, 1914). For this reason alone, therefore, we should conclude that, if the anaclitic-narcissistic distinction is to be retained as of use for psychoanalytical thought, it will require thoroughgoing reformulation.

It is in this context that the writing of Klein may briefly be considered. Therein both the distinctions between the aim and object, and narcissistic and anaclitic object-choice are set aside in consequence of her conception of unconscious phantasy. A number of proposals are entered in this regard (this account of Kleinian theory will be highly condensed, as my sole purpose is to suggest why male same-sex desire cannot but be pathological for the Kleinian variant of psychoanalytic thought. For a scholarly elucidation of the major concepts of Kleinian theory, see Hinshelwood, 1989). As the infant's 'rudimentary' ego is related to two part-objects from the outset of post-uterine life, he experiences an ideal breast as the source of all 'goodness' and a 'bad' breast as a function of the projection of the death instinct. Now add that the newborn enters the world with innate 'knowledge' of the anatomical distinction between the sexes and of the roles the penis and vagina play in human reproduction. Finally, negotiation of the travails of depressive functioning – in particular, the capacity for reparation – depends in part on mitigating the fantasy of the violent intercourse of the 'combined parent figure'. When this mitigation succeeds, the 'creativity' of parental intercourse can be internalized (Klein, 1946; Hinshelwood, 1989; Likierman, 2000).

On this portrayal of the transformation of psychically organized impulses consequent upon depressive functioning, male same-sex desire cannot but be pathological. As numerous commentators, including those who contributed to the Controversial Discussions of the early 1940s, have noted, the key to Kleinian thought in this connection is the attribution of sophisticated innate knowledge to the infant, in combination with the thesis that a rudimentary ego, existing from the first days of postpartum life, first relates to a mother's breast bifurcated by projected destructiveness. On this account, same-sex desire is the child of hostility and envy – specifically, of the gay man's hatred of the reproductive creativity of heterosexual erotic love. Although we can appreciate that it is possible to think so when heterosexuality is taken as the normative psychical outcome, the revision of Freudian thought at issue has been purchased at an exorbitant price. In place of the aim-object distinction we have a 'relational' thesis superintended by what is, frankly speaking, theoretical heterosexism, as this brief text of Hanna Segal's makes plain:

> I think that there is some reality sense and some innate idea about the parental couple and creative sexuality which is attacked by homosexuality.
>
> (Segal, cited in O'Connor and Ryan, 1993, p. 89)

How are we to respond to that claim? Whereas Freud is certainly incoherent on the question of male homosexuality, Klein's theory of psychical development depends on a thoroughgoing 'heterosexualization' of all erotic love. In addition, the privilege Klein accords parental intercourse as the 'real' awaiting internalization relies on accepting two beliefs most psychoanalytical clinicians today would not endorse. First, 'homosexuals' constitute a discrete, unified group of men. Freud did not believe so, and nor did Stoller (1975); indeed, the latter has advised, as has Stubrin (1994) that psychoanalysis has been mistaken in drawing a global distinction between heterosexuality and homosexuality. Accuracy demands that we conceive of hetero- and homosexualities in the plural. Second, object choice alone for Kleinian thought can be taken as a sign of underlying 'pathology'. Again, Freud and Stoller disagreed, as does Stubrin (ibid.). In passing, another point is worth making: if the Kleinian psychoanalyst is to be consistent, there is nothing the gay man could possibly say which would persuade his analyst that his desire is not fuelled by hatred directed to the sexual union to which he owes his life.

Let us inquire now, why should we continue to believe that psychoanalysis, as represented by Freud and Klein at least, has anything of lasting value to contribute to our understanding of same-sex desire? Freud's reproductivist bias, together with the homophobia of so much post-Freudian psychoanalytical theory (Lewes, ibid.), has blocked the engagement we could justifiably have expected from his thesis of the object's variability. And Kleinian theory's heterosexism is (partly) the product of its abolition of the aim–object distinction. But we must consider the work of Stoller in more detail before reaching any definitive conclusion, since he has supported yet simultaneously re-envisioned Freud's distinction between the aim and the object by uniting the hetero- and homosexualities. Unlike the 'perversions', Stoller has argued, the hetero- and homosexualities are not characterized by the desire for revenge upon the traumatizing primary object (Stoller, 1975).

What are the implications of this re-conceptualization? Although the marriage of male same-sex desire and practice is statistically deviant in our culture, while it was not so in the Greco-Roman imperium, it can be, and in the vast majority of cases probably is, as psychodynamically unexceptional as the desire for the heterogenital embrace. This is where Freud's note in *The Essays* apropos the Greeks becomes pertinent. As Stoller and Stubrin have independently noted, psychoanalysis has conflated statistical deviance and psychical 'pathology' because its accounts of same-sex desire have (inevitably) been based on insignificant samples of highly distressed gay men. In other words, what the psychoanalyst knows of homoerotic pleasure cannot be generalized to gay men as a whole. That being so, Freud's note can productively be read as a warning directed to those coming after him: take care, he is advising, since the ancient Greeks furnish an example of how a specific kind of 'inversion', one based on the educative practices and political ideals of the time, can be normative, at least among a citizen elite. Furthermore (our imaginary Freud continues), the Greek experience shows us that the reproduction of our species can carry on irrespective of how many men find the male body of erotic interest. In sum, we can imagine Freud day-dreaming to the effect that if same-sex desire can be culturally endorsed yet the human species continue to thrive, flirtation with bad Darwinism will ruin the radical potential of psychoanalytical suspicion.

This fancy aside, Stoller knows, as did Freud, that it has been a serious error – perhaps a cruelty too, in Richard Rorty's sense of the term (Rorty, 1989) (we are being 'cruel', according to Rorty, when we refuse to extend to 'others' the privileges, rights and so forth that we are fortunate to enjoy under the conditions of advanced liberal democracy) – to think that object-choice is necessarily connected with the relations between the id, ego and superego among those whom identify as gay men. To which we may add, in light of the history of theoretical revision in psychoanalysis, that it is unsurprising that we remain so ignorant today of what any of the hetero- and homosexualities might have in common in respect of the quality of relationships they seek, and can sustain.

The limits of hope

It has often been said that we live in a time in which confidence in universalizing, global accounts of social-historical relations has been lost. Certainly, Marxism has lost its power to enthrall many of us, and the master-voice of theoretical reason has fragmented partly because feminist scholarship has advised that there is no escape from the motivated character of our theoretical claims. Two other developments merit brief note. Firstly, the form of historical writing, genealogy, which Foucault has deployed in the first volume of *The History of Sexuality* (1981, hereafter HS) has proceeded by bracketing the category of the human subject. Since the object of inquiry of HS is the manner in which sexology, psychiatry and psychoanalysis have subjectified us by virtue of sexuality, Foucault deliberately suspends the categories of consciousness, Man [*sic*], ideology and psyche in order to interrogate the subjectification effects of such discourses. And, second, the work of the historian and philosopher of science, Thomas Kuhn, has alerted us to the possibly incommensurable character of the various modes of inquiry available to us for conceiving of the good tomorrow (Kuhn, 1962).

Now, as a function of the different histories of interest to them, genealogy and psychoanalysis make radically conflicting claims about modern subjectivity. The history at stake in HS is one of 'events' that cannot be traced to the operation of any principle of causality – to the powers of the capitalist mode of production (Marxism), for example, or of 'society' as a functioning system (some sociology). Rather, what has appeared in modern historical time is a series of 'accidents' that despite their contingency have issued in the effects of subjectification we live today. Subjects *of* the sexual apparatus and subject *to* it, we now identify ourselves and others on the basis of erotic desire. On this account, different forms of subjectivity have appeared in historical time, so much so that although we share an anxiety concerning same-sex desire with the ancient Greeks, we are little like them in numerous other ways (Foucault, 1986).

And psychical history: it is not an 'external' history howsoever written that is of interest to psychoanalysis. Psychoanalytical inquiry not only addresses the universally operating 'internal' processes responsible for, as Freud once put it, being able to love and work without disabling inhibition; it posits (in different ways) that 'beneath' the conscious mental activity of all human subjects lies the domain of unconscious functioning. That noted, we can now identify why genealogy and psychoanalysis are incommensurable. Genealogy thinks of psychoanalysis as the quintessential mode of modern inquiry that, by means of the category of the psychic unconscious, essentializes subjectivity. Hence why Foucault, in using historical materials for the double purpose of pointing to how different we are from our forbears and making us strange to ourselves, eschews consciousness and its conceptual cognate – the psychic unconscious – as an analytical tool. By doing so, his various genealogies have advanced the analysis of the discursive effects responsible for who we are today. As for psychoanalysis, because it is first and foremost a therapeutic practice, it must infer the operation of unconscious agency from the patient's speech and, on that basis, construct its accounts of the psychical processes responsible for the production of human subjectivity *tout court*.

'What has this to do with the limits of hope?' we may ask now. A great deal, in fact. Foucault spoke of 'creating our sexuality' in an interview conducted towards the end of his life. Leaving aside for the moment the voluntarism apparent in that remark, what it suggests is that it could have been otherwise had the sexual apparatus not colonized the erotic terrain of our time. Furthermore, because 'heterosexual' and 'homosexual' are names, but also identity markers fashioned by the apparatus, they may well disappear one day. How could they do so? Well, that is up to us – presumably to a sexual politics capable of transforming our erotic landscape. This claim chimes with the analytical method Foucault deploys in HS: materials – records, books, the architecture of buildings, and so on – are examined in the light of a question or problem posed to the 'archive', rather than treated as 'expressions' of a general principle of causality governing the social-historical domain. Accordingly, it could be argued that Foucault has done much to acquaint us with what will be possible in the future. Because all that is at stake is the disappearance of names, the heterosexual-homosexual game of modern powers will prove readily changeable.

Before we subscribe to that judgement, however, two – I believe, decisive – qualifications must be made. One springs from Foucault's work on governmentality and his vision of the local intellectual, the other from psychoanalysis. On the first count, 'heterosexual' and 'homosexual' are far more than fragile names easily to be dispatched to the dustbin of history by force of a collective act of will. They are operating categories enmeshed in a plethora of modern regulatory practices, including legal statutes, psychiatry, psychology, social work, and, more broadly, in our therapeutic culture. Unless therefore we wish to invent some fabulous successor to the ruined revolutionary apocalypse of the Marxist imaginary, progress will be slow in transforming our present. This is not to say that HS is of little political value, but it is to believe that historical inventions can be no less 'real' for all that they have only lately appeared on the scene of action.

The best in psychoanalysis supports this judgement. From the psycho-analytical point of view, 'heterosexual' and 'homosexual' are best understood as the rendezvous points for complex psychical processes issuing in erotic object-choice – in what we nowadays call sexual identity. And albeit that psychoanalysis's record on same-sex desire has been lamentable, what it advises of a human subjectivity born of trauma usefully undermines our more utopian visions of what will be politically feasible over the next three generations or so. Think of this possibility: if the writing of Stoller were to become better known, even such a welcome development would do little to change the obstacles to transforming our present. Most of us, so I like to think, would be kinder to men-loving men, as a result of taking Stoller on board; kinder, in the knowledge that all forms of 'mature' sexual desire and practice spring from the same psychical roots. That would be a civilizing change worth having, although it will not have changed the range of erotic identity markers available to us today.

Conclusion

From where, then, will hope come? We will not find it, this much seems clear, if we believe that a psychoanalysis fit for the modern world can be used to change the psychical processes upon which it reports. Arguably, psychoanalysis's powers of transformation are limited to the therapeutic experience it has made possible; all else is windy speculation, of no use to political calculation and action. Nor will we find hope if, along with the more voluntaristic of Foucault's claims, we think of sexuality with some omnipotent fantasy of 'self'-creation in tow. The sexual apparatus is still there, still having its effects on us, still making possible the tradition against which some of our children will protest.

From where will hope come? Perhaps Gramsci's dictum, 'pessimism of the intellect, optimism of the will' will serve us well.

8
The Fear of Male Humiliation

Tessa Adams

I have been out on the moors for about a week now, this is an endurance exercise. Temperatures are below freezing, rations are light and there is no cooked food. It is 6.30 a.m. Relieved, cold and starving, I am called back to base. On arrival, I am greeted by the delicious smell of bacon. Believing that I am going to be fed at last, I eagerly greet the Corporal. 'Like some bacon Stevens?', he asks, 'Yes Sir', I answer with anticipation. 'Kneel down and open your mouth' he commands and with my mouth wide open I drop to me knees. A piece of bacon is dangled before me, taking it in I attempt to close my mouth to chew, but a second order comes – 'Keep that mouth wide open, Stevens – there is more'. Opening my mouth, still kneeling, I wait; then the shock hits me, for what follows is not more bacon but the solidifying fat from the pan. Gulping and enraged I stand up, spit it out, and glancing over my shoulder as I walk away I deliver my message, a warning, with vengeance – 'There will come a time, Corporal.'

Craig Stevens is now a Colour Sergeant acting as a leading armourer representing his regiment in war. In the past, Bosnia and the Gulf proved a demanding training ground and recently Iraq has tested him. He has become a crack shot, and not only is he skilled in weapon maintenance; he has also achieved considerable respect as a marksman in Marine field events by winning several trophies. The experience described above was relayed to me directly. I had asked men from different professions to consider a proposition that I wished to investigate, namely, that it is men's humiliation of men which engenders male violence. In presenting this proposition to the men I interviewed, in each case there appeared to be a keenness to relay humiliating experiences of equal brutality (as Craig's) which had been remembered with strikingly vivid recall.

A factor of Craig's experience, which rendered it all the more shocking, was that since boyhood Craig had longed to be accepted into Marine training. Growing up in Plymouth, a city that celebrates Marines as the elite force, Craig had come to respect and internalize the Marine as the exemplification of responsible manhood. More significantly, this positive view of manhood had been compensatory for Craig who found male leadership in his upbringing to be lacking. Yet this initiation into his training which purported to test his endurance, rather than reinforcing this long held respect, alarmed and unsettled Craig instigating his determination not to be so naively ridiculed again. Thus Craig learnt, in the moment of the Corporal's triumph through both humiliation and disillusionment, that military authorities could not be trusted.

In further discussion over the incident, Craig explained that the term for permitted practices of training humiliation (such as the one that he had described) is *beasting*. This 'catch all' term signifies accepted bullying as a practice which all training Marines come to fear. That is to say, the term 'beasting' stands for a Senior Officer's legitimized punishment of ratings for either the purposes of training or for insignificant misdemeanours. Craig, now as a Non-Commissioned Officer, inevitably has taken up the mantle. When asked about his own actions, dropping his head and averting his eyes, Craig admitted to his own part in this bullying practice with the explanation, 'I do far less beasting than other N.C.Os.'

Psychoanalysis and male humiliation

Turning to the psychoanalytic understanding of humiliating practices, what becomes transparent here is that while there is certainly considerable attention to the status of self-esteem in counselling and psychoanalytic practice, the attention to the effects of humiliation seems to be wanting. For example, in searching for references to humiliation, including the index of the *Standard Edition* of Freud's works, I was concerned to find that there is a paucity of direct attention to 'humiliation' as such in psychoanalytic literature. Freud (1911) does mention, however, humiliation when commenting on paranoid mechanisms stating: 'the strikingly prominent features in the causation of paranoia, especially among males, are social humiliations and slights' (p. 60).

What has been much discussed is that Freud indicates that the means by which the Oedipal conflict for the infant boy is resolved is through the anxiety of castration being mitigated via identification with the potential aggressor, conceived by Freud as the father who institutes prohibition and law. But what seems to be overlooked is that Freud does not clarify fully whether castration anxiety is firmly attached to the prospect of corporeal loss or the psychological estrangement that it signifies.

In other words, is castration anxiety (engendered during the infantile psycho-sexual development and unconsciously present in adulthood) simply about the robbing of a body part, or is its primary effectiveness derived from the prospect of the robbing of status? And if so, is the potency of this infantile challenge, which furnishes the Oedipal neurosis, exceeded by the psychological dimension of the fear of humiliation that would accompany the fantasized visceral loss? Clearly, Freudian theory signifies that the fear of castration is founded both in actual and symbolic reality, yet it is predominantly the fear of loss of the body part that is cited as the haunting trajectory that furnishes the boy's identification with male potency. As Laplanche and Pontalis (1983) point out, the resolution of the Oedipal conflict brings with it 'the emergence of such feelings as shame and disgust along with aesthetic aspirations' (p. 54).

It is useful to consider here, and perhaps generally relevant, the suggestion that the fear of humiliation is synonymous with the fear of castration, since it can be readily argued that to be humiliated is frequently presented as a form of symbolic castration. Yet if the fear of castration refers primarily to the fantasized risk of the loss of the literal body part within the drama of the Oedipal conflict of infancy, the implication is that humiliating practices derive their libidinal potency from unconscious primitive anxieties. If this is the case, it could be argued that what draws the individual to perpetrate humiliating practices (and derive gratification from these acts) is precisely the need to project the internalized fantasies of castration which furnished those early infantile fears of loss, the potency of which will thereby become enhanced by the guilt of forbidden desire. Within this scenario the original infantile anxiety of castration will be primarily compensated by the potential achievement of superiority. Thus, if there is a relationship between the anxiety of humiliation and the need for superiority, then it would seem appropriate that psychoanalytic literature would address both the manifestation of humiliating practices and the impact of such experiences (as those expressed by Craig).

It is interesting to acknowledge that where the concerns about humiliating processes (in recent years) has been located within the practice of psychoanalysis has been predominantly in relation to gender and race, with the view that the Eurocentric bias of the psychoanalytic profession needed to be addressed. And in particular much has been written on what is arguably Freud's asymmetrical analysis of the infant's resolution of the Oedipal crisis. That is to say, while contemporary psychoanalytic critique appears to address the issues of gender and race in terms of repudiation, the fundamental attention to humiliating practices per se (as an integral aspect of social practice) seems to have been left, by and large, unchallenged. Thus, I would argue that there remains a central thesis to be addressed in terms of the insistent evidence that the fascination with humiliating practices preoccupies many aspects of society as a means of determining power relations and, more specifically, in the destabilization of maleness.

In the light of the questions that have been outlined above, it would be helpful to turn to the entertainment industry, since there is no doubt that much of comedy rests on the staging of the humiliation of the male. In other words, the evidence of the male, cast as victim to be ridiculed furnishes the entertainment industry without significant censorship. We only have to think of the common player within this scenario, namely, the male 'stooge', who typically is cast as he who can withstand many forms of humiliation that would normally enrage most adult males. Laurel and Hardy, Chaplin and Keaton, for example, occupy iconic status for just such fictional representations of their ability to transcend humiliation. Furthermore, 'Reality TV' programmes which are currently broadcast widely and consistently maintain top ratings, draw significant audiences from the view that libidinal gratification will be gained (by the viewer) from the permitted humiliation of the participants. The question to be raised here is whether or not the cultural forms of comedy and media presentations of humiliating practice serve, consciously or subliminally, as a form of catharsis that is designed to mitigate the prospect that human engagement for the male will revisit the original trajectory of castration anxiety.

The view that comedy offers catharsis is explored by Freud (1905) in his study of jokes, humour and mimicry. Freud focuses on the cost of 'libidinal expenditure' in his attempts to make a case for the psychological investment in comedy and joking. The comic, we are told, can play with the prospect of humiliation without engendering our feelings of superiority. For should he or she purposefully stumble and fall so as to amuse, this is very different from the literal repudiated stumbling in life. As Freud explains humour frames the act as a process of pretence and thereby the dynamic of humiliation is mitigated. Freud also looks at caricature and parody as a means by which the exalted is degraded and he demonstrates that such methods of illusionary humiliating practice become the scaffold by which repudiation can be publicly witnessed.

Notwithstanding Freud's discussion of humiliation in relation to comedy and parody, there is still little discussion of the problematic of humiliation within everyday life. In this light, I find it significant that Charles Rycroft appears to beg the question that concerns us here, namely, the lack of representation of the impact of the psychology of humiliation within psychoanalytic discourse. In his Second Edition of the *Critical Dictionary of Psychoanalysis*, he ventures, as one of the few psychoanalysts, to offer an entry under the heading 'Humiliation', with the purpose of addressing the issue that there has been a certain level of neglect (within psychoanalytic thinking) in respect of the affects of humiliating practices. Rycroft points to Kohut as a psychoanalytic theorist who understands this problematic, namely, that humiliation can be perceived as a direct attack on the ego, and worse, that the affect is lasting in that certain aspects of humiliation instigate a legacy of narcissistic wounding. Rycroft's entry is as follows:

> **Humiliation:** In psychoanalytical language, humiliating experiences are 'injuries to the ego' and *narcissistic wounds*. Responses to humiliation are hate and narcissistic rage. The assumption of both classical and Kleinian theory that hate is an instinct has led to neglect of the importance of humiliation as a cause of hatred, but see Kohut (1972).
>
> (Rycroft, 1975, p. 71)

What Kohut emphasizes within this paper of 1972 is that feelings of humiliation spring from narcissistic wounding which in turn trigger what he terms 'archaic rage'. In other words, Kohut focuses on the capacities of the ego and puts forward a theory of retaliation that has as its root both the internalized original hurt of infancy and externalized shaming of the adult exchange. Arguably Kohut recognizes that humiliating acts inevitably find the chinks in the ego's armour where there has been an original failure of security in early nurturing. In other words, the affect of insecurity instituted within adult functioning makes it possible for a re-enactment of primitive retaliation to become manifest in the context of humiliating experience. Put simply, Kohut indicates that there is a relationship between an individual's ego strength and the ability to bear the hurts of shaming. This position is based upon Kohut's view that retributive acts are the product of that which cannot be reconciled where the individual, during infancy, had suffered narcissistic wounding that remains a vital sore to be touched upon throughout the vicissitudes of adulthood.

Thus, this becomes a cautionary tale since what Kohut underlines with regard to aggressive processes being harnessed to frame human courage, is the prospect that negative outcomes, arising from humiliating practices, will be ever present. As evidenced, there is little doubt (as mentioned above) that in the context of a social/cultural perspective humiliating practices have been considered to be an aspect of power relations, not least during the 1970s when certain feminist theories located the humiliation of women both in relationship to men and in the prejudicial view of feminine inferiority. Thus, the feminism of that period was clearly exercised with the concern that deep psychological distress for many women derived from the reality of women suffering humiliation through discriminatory societal practices. Certainly in terms of racial prejudicial practices, such as slavery, and homophobic legislation, many men also have met the societal prejudices of a similar nature as those operating for women. But in the past, arguably, what has not been addressed fully is the proposition that it is men, within a democratic society, who fear humiliation more consistently than women, and that this issue is yet to be explored analytically. Freud, as mentioned above, alludes to this in relation to his concern with the paranoid personality when he points out that manifestations of psychosis owe much to the wounds of 'social humiliations' and specifically 'in the case of men'. What I am suggesting here is that humiliating practices operate across a broad arena of male experience, and, in this light, it cannot be ruled out that males of contemporary society may still be drawn to develop their own form of 'beasting' when achieving the position of power; the legacy of which is engendered by certain aspects of humiliating exposure during boyhood/adolescence.

A further leading question that can be raised is, why is it that psychoanalytic literature appears to be competent to discuss 'shame' while avoiding the discussion of the process of 'shaming', since shaming is the agency of humiliating practice? In other words, the individual feeling shame or ashamed is readily approached psychoanalytically, while the practice of the shaming of the other appears to be largely neglected.

As we have seen Rycroft, citing Kohut, raises the issue that if hate is seen in classical Freudian or Kleinian terms to solely derive from instinct, then the social/relational agency of hate will remain unaddressed. Clearly, this has implications in terms of how we see aggressive acts whether they are institutionalized (as in the case of war) or individualized. For if aggressive behaviour is seen as simply arising from an instinctual need for gratification which, if acted out denotes lack of socialization, then the responsibility towards aggressive behaviour will be identified as the province of social control, namely, law. This is to suggest that in the case of war, if the urgency for violence is deemed instinctual, and thereby largely unconsciously charged, then to mitigate such violence could only be tempered by prohibition in terms of sanctions, and possibly more aggression. But if war is seen to be driven by external factors that influence instinctual demands, such as humiliating practices, then the question of mitigation would indicate the prospect of preventative measures that would reference unconscious demand, on the one hand, while diminishing the prospect of retaliation, on the other. This is to suggest that if humiliating practices are seen to access instinctual aggression, then the project of reducing rather than enhancing combative conflict (such as war) could be informed by the analyses that seek to understand the interrelationship between primary aggression and social shaming – humiliation.

This proposition (namely that humiliation engenders humiliating practices) is borne out in the way in which Craig threatened his humiliator – 'there will come a time Corporal'. Of course *that* time never came; rather it was the Marine rhetoric of 'beasting' (a permitted violence against juniors) that offered up the compensatory beasting of surrogates. Of course, as with Craig, these surrogates would in turn take up the prospect of furthering these permitted humiliating processes as part of their eventual advancement and promotion. Thus, when the press deem the possibility that the Geneva Convention has been violated by the Military, it is the public and the politicians who seem to be surprised, while the Senior Military offer reprisals in the form of further law as the means by which to curb the inchoate passions believing them to be, in the future, held in check. What is more surprising is that a training that 'beasts' would not be identified as a training that would enculture the 'beast'.

In order to emphasize the concerns raised thus far, I will offer a further example that directly depends upon male experience and reports of humiliating practices furnishing further humiliating acts. The context of this example is a community project designed to help those in alcohol recovery situated in South East London. The catchment of this project consisted of a residential group of men who met on a daily basis as a support group with the task of giving up entrenched alcohol use. It was suggested to the therapist, at a time when the group had become morose and fairly uncooperative, that she asked each participant to recall a humiliating experience. What surprised the facilitator was that each individual within the group collaborated without reserve with a ready example to proffer. Furthermore, a consistent feature of the exchanges within the session was that all the participants presented not only an example, with considerable detail of their own humiliating experience, but individually countered their recall of humiliation with an anecdote of how they in turn had humiliated the perpetrator as a form of reprisal. What this suggests is that each of the participants chose to present a case which would allow them to both locate a personal distressful humiliating experience, yet were eager to regain status by demonstrating how they themselves could 'beast' in return. In other words, unable to stay with the feelings of humiliation that still remained, the participant sought to gain standing from the group, first, by indicating that they were capable of surviving, and, second, by demonstrating that they could equally mete out humiliating acts.

The issue at stake here is whether or not humiliating practices that are historically and currently located within the male community (and for the male community) engender violence. Clearly, the struggle to endure and resist humiliation both in the case of the marine and in the reports of the group mentioned above indicates that the drive for the reinstatement of prestige is evidenced by the way that humiliating experience is recalled in which both shaming and reprisal are juxtaposed. It is possible that this juxtaposition of the subject of repudiation and the object of the repudiated, limits the prospect of completion. For if the one who is humiliated is seen to have a right of reprisal, then the prospect of resolution becomes exponential. In other words, the humiliating act will engender further humiliating enactment, which in turn submits the human subject to meet all violation violently. This is no more evident than in the conflict zones of the World.

If it is clear that shame and shaming remain the co-ordinates of humiliation and humiliation engenders (in the male) violence then what needs to be addressed is the revisioning of male-to-male power relationships. At the feet of his instructor and at the peak of his endurance, Craig was vulnerable and expectant. Such was this spectacle of youth, enthusiasm and physical prowess that the beasting was, in this context, designed to challenge his exuberance. Clearly, institutionalizing shaming as the fulcrum of transition to manhood is in question. In the past humiliating rituals (such as the tarring and feathering of the apprentice) were deemed acceptable ensuring that boyhood be forfeited at a cost, namely, the achievement of manhood would be claimed through fear and suppression. It seems that this hard bargain is still being made. Yet, there have been times when Marines have become an issue for media coverage in terms of the 'beasting' rituals for new trainees. Images of naked youths fighting and being humiliated by both the nakedness and inability to conquer their opponent have raised questions as to the bestial nature of training practices. As one Senior Officer stated,

> There are certain rituals within Marine training that are purposefully designed to prepare the initiatives for the onslaught of war which should stay within the boundary of what is acceptable, but where

this is transgressed and this form of preparation for war exceeds what is acceptable, then the law should intercede.

(ITV News – Nov. 05)

From statements such as this a paradox is offered, for we can see that a certain level of acceptable humiliation is conceived as a tool for maturation in respect of engendering the masculine concept of courage and fortitude. However, there is always the prospect that such practices can undermine to such an extent that those who internalize fear rather than develop the courage expected of them will receive the humiliating rituals as abusive. That is to say, there is no doubt that certain trainees will experience these ritualistic aggressive practices as a form of intimidation.

Thus, it appears that a fine line is drawn, not only to denote that which can forge the male character, as soldier, marine or mercenary, but that which marks out the prospect of failure in terms of human frailty – namely the prospect of humiliating practice. What this means, in psychological terms, is that the training of Marines rests on both the premise of narcissistic engrandisment, on the one hand, and its disillusionment, on the other. Clearly, this has implications for both the clinic and for the military, since in either case the subject is asked to both forfeit and to reinforce the attachment to the ideal. In the military, this may seem to be a simplistic project, since that which is seen to sustain prestige is continuously challenged. But in the context of the clinic the fear of humiliation becomes that which was always feared in primitive terms from infancy (castration) and that which can occur through narcissistic wounding in adulthood. Within the military reprisal eventually will be gained through warfare, but within the community reprisal becomes that which cannot be institutionalized (as in the case of the soldier preparing for battle). Instead the prospect of the perversion of power manifests through the enculturation of intimidation.

Humiliation and the making of masculinity

Now, to return to the suggestion that processing humiliating experiences may well be generally more intensely experienced by men than by women. This could clearly be seen to be a polemical proposition, yet in asking men to relate humiliating experience, I witnessed a certain level of vivid recall that typified the vignettes that were given. Furthermore, as has been already mentioned, it is clear that the Military uses humiliating practices as the agency of developing 'masculine courage'. This is not to say that there have not been examples of humiliating practices used in the training of women, but more significantly these come less readily to mind; equally the prospect of aggression in its severest forms is statistically attributed to men. James Gilligan (2000), a prison psychiatrist, in his research on the psychology of violence, certainly supports this assumption and purposefully addresses the relationship between shaming and aggression in what he terms 'the making of masculinity'.

Gilligan focuses on violence and in particular the motives of men who admit to have committed horrifying crimes rather than bear a loss of self-respect. His writing emphasizes the role that shame occupies in the etiology of murder. Mapping his clinical interventions with criminals who apparently show no remorse, Gilligan reveals underlying narratives of humiliating experiences that occupied the childhood and adolescence of the men whom he analyses. Gilligan's position is more behavioural than psychoanalytic, yet in the questions that he raises as to fear of shaming he parallel's Freud's analysis of the fear of castration by suggesting that at root it is the genital potency of the male that is protected against repudiation. He states that it is the literal act of 'castration (or emasculation) and rape [that] are the two most powerful ways of inflicting ultimate shame and humiliation on another person' (Cilligan, 2000, p. 151). Quoting a statement by Mark Twain that 'man is the only animal that blushes', Gilligan forwards his thesis that 'Humankind is the only animal that feels shame'. From this position, Gilligan emphasizes his claim that both the avoidance and the result of humiliation engender violence. As he states:

> Men will often kill or assault each other in the struggle to avoid being in the submissive position, and experience an almost bottomless sense of degradation – when they do submit – to the point where, effectively their self has died.
>
> (ibid., p. 152)

Furthermore, Gilligan proposes that there is an interrelationship between experiences of submission and sexual identity. He lays emphasis on the fear of genital shaming by using such phrases that report the public exposure of humiliation as seeming as if the person is 'being caught with [his] pants down' (ibid., p. 153). There is much in Gilligan's work that echoes the prospect that shaming can be used as a tool to forge violence, which appears to be validated by the military employing the process of shaming such as 'beasting' in order to stimulate the prospect of a rating's future gladiatorial engagement. Gilligan's example is of a form of humiliating practice meted out to initiates on entering prison.

He reports of the new entrant being purposefully exposed in the form of stripping down and suffering the humiliation of anal investigation. As Gilligan emphasizes, while the legitimization of this practice is purportedly to check for disease, the fact that it is done in front other initiates and senior officers (that are not medics) indicates that the ambition to subject the new entrant to the most humiliating exposure is designed to reinforce the power differential.

Gilligan's work and research have led to his concern about the roles that manhood is socially permitted to take. He discusses the male 'code of honour' which presents passive engagement as dishonourable, stating, 'Men are honoured for activity (ultimately, violent activity) and they are dishonoured for passivity (or pacifism) which renders them to the charge of being a non-man' (ibid., p. 231). In taking a historical perspective Gilligan attempts to change the behaviour of some of the most violent criminals that are imprisoned both in literal terms and in terms of their terror of relinquishing violence. He offers a summary of the problem (gained from years of understanding the male psyche and the defence against loss of face) when he states,

> I have yet to see a serious act of violence that is not predicated by the experience of feeling shamed and humiliated, disrespected and ridiculed and did not represent the attempt to prevent or undo this 'loss of face' – no matter how severe the punishment, even if includes death.
>
> (ibid., p. 110)

Clearly Gilligan does not suggest that these conditions operate for all men. Similarly to Kohut what he is keen to emphasize is that where the conditions in upbringing, social status and well-being have resulted in narcissistic wounding from an early age then the prospect of belonging, and a sense of being loved and being able to love can be overwhelmed by the anxiety of being humiliated. Thus, he states that 'when a man feels sufficiently impotent and humiliated, the usual assumptions one makes about human behaviour and motivation no longer hold' (ibid., p. 110). Gilligan encapsulates the perversion of violence on which 'beasting' rests. Craig's warning 'There will come a time Corporal' is ever present in Gilligan's view where humiliation is purposefully meted out. Of one of his patients who murdered and was interned (to meet a death sentence) Gilligan offers a chilling warning since in this case the justification for murdering is reflected in the prisoner's reasoning for retaliation. Significantly, the prisoner's explanation is of a symbolic death through an accumulation of familial humiliations that primed the violence of his acts of slaughter. His confession rings of an insurmountable experience psychological wounding in claiming that, 'The people I murdered had murdered me. They murdered me slow like. I was better to them. I killed them in a hurry' (ibid., p. 37). What this 'slow like murder' was referring to was a lifetime of psychological abuse founded on humiliation. Unfortunately the law prevailed, since the state ironically furnished a furthering 'coming of a time' as the response to literal murder on death row (taking no account of psychological 'death') could only barter a further literal execution.

Conclusion

I will end with a reference to the sixteenth century that indicates contrasting imperatives of conduct for men and women. The directive is from Castiglione (1528) who distinguished the appropriate forms of deportment in gendered terms. And what seems apparent (from the assumptions of this advice) is that lack of strength and virility in a male was to be repudiated. Thus, the split between men and women, in terms of virility and strength and passivity and gentleness that Gilligan has underlined, has been instituted historically. Furthermore, it is the forms of gesture that Castiglione profiled that influenced the ways that women and men were to be depicted through the paintings of the Renaissance and Baroque periods – much of which contributed to the features of masculinity and femininity today. I quote,

> just as it behoves him [the man] to display a certain firm and steady virility, so it is fitting for her [the woman] to possess a soft and delicate tenderness, with a feminine sweetness in her every movement, so that everything in her walking, standing, and speaking whatever she will, pronounces her as woman, with no resemblance to man.
>
> (Castiglione, 1528, p. 341)

9
Achieving Our Country: Ethnic Difference and White Men's Racism

Larry O'Carroll

By considering the case of white men's racism vis-à-vis black men, one of the aims of this chapter is to explore the explanatory limits of psychoanalysis in comparison with anthropology. As we shall see, the different explanatory strengths of psychoanalysis and anthropology must be borne in mind when assessing the possibility of achieving a better, less racist, country. In focusing on white-black racism, moreover, it is not my intention to imply that a particular instance of in-group/out-group relations characterized by anxieties antithetical to the achievement of a more inclusive country is somehow more unacceptable than any other. Rather, the chapter is concerned with white men's racism because it exemplifies why attending to psychical processes does not account for why black men have become and remain, if to a lesser extent than say thirty years ago, a racialized social category in contemporary Western societies (see Dalal, 2002). Furthermore, anthropology's concern with how the culturally instituted fashions human subjectivity does not explain what arguably fuels all racisms irrespective of the historical times and cultural locations of their appearance – namely, how wounding marginalization can set in train certain psychical processes, given always particular social-historical conditions.

The chapter has a subsidiary aim. Despite anti-discrimination legislation and educational practices informed by multiculturalist ethics, many young black men in the Western world have bonded together in what sociologists used to call a 'subculture'. For what reason have they done so? In large part, surely so as to resist the racism to which they have been, and continue to be, subjected, despite legislation and educational policies informed by a fundamental multiculturalist insistence. By right of our equality as citizens of a liberal democracy worth the name, all of us are entitled to dignity and respect; to the same redress as well, when any 'other' – be it an individual, an educational institution or governmental agency – fails to do so. As welcome as such bonding may be, however, and although it may have provided something approaching a 'secure base' to the racialized from which to forge identities in contestation of racist significations and practices, it is a worrying, and dangerous, development.

The psychoanalysis of racism

Since the late 1920s when Bronislav Malinowski became disenchanted with the reception his anthropological analysis of the 'nuclear complex' (the Oedipus) among the Trobriand Islanders received from Ernest Jones, many anthropologists and sociologists have argued that psychoanalysis is incapable of addressing how the practices and beliefs of particular cultures fashion different kinds of human subjectivity (Malinowski 1937; Jones 1964). Malinowski was among the first to insist that psychoanalysis and the post-evolutionist anthropology he had played a singular role in creating were irrevocably opposed in their theoretical and methodological assumptions. In retrospect, we can read him as having anticipated the career of psychoanalysis in relation to the human sciences: their forms of inquiry cannot be married (Foucault, 1970; Hirst and Woolley, 1982). Yet, that is neither to say that psychoanalysis is 'just' a discourse, a 'point of view', but a local, 'western' way of conceiving of how human subjectivity is organized in culture; nor, against Malinowski and, more recently, Gellner (1981), is it to advise that psychoanalysis, in comparison with anthropology, owes far more to religious dogmatics than it has thus far been willing to admit. Nevertheless, there are two limits to what any psychoanalytical account of racism can achieve. One limit has to do with the penchant psychoanalytical thought of all varieties has shown for obliterating historical time and cultural particularity because of its concern with the psychical processes responsible for the birth of human subjects; the other with its temptation to think that claims licensed by its therapeutic method retain their epistemological character when applied to extra-clinical phenomena like racism.

Many years after Malinowski's disenchantment with psychoanalytical inquiry, Claude Levi-Strauss, the founder of structuralist anthropology, advised of social constraint and the relations between customs and sentiments, in these terms:

> Social constraints, whether positive or negative, cannot be explained, either in their origin or in their persistence, as the effects of

impulses or emotions which appear again and again, with the same characteristics and during the course of centuries and millennia, in different individuals. ... [A]s far as the present is concerned, it is certain that social behaviour is not produced spontaneously by each individual, under the influence of the emotions of the present. ... Customs are given as external norms before giving rise to internal sentiments, and these non-sentient norms determine the sentiments of individuals as well as the circumstances in which they may, or must, be displayed.

(Levi-Strauss, 1964, pp. 69–70)

Levi-Strauss here implicitly chides Freud, all subsequent psychoanalytical thought too, for what, from the anthropological perspective, is its reduction of social institutions, those assemblies of multiple 'constraint', to the 'effects of impulses or emotions' of individual psyches. This reductionism has a direct bearing on how we are to understand racism. Since racisms are, to use a term of Castoriadis's, in part born of social-historical significations, they are irreducible to individuals' beliefs, wishes, anxieties and other intentional states (Castoriadis, 1984). Methodologically speaking, therefore, unless anthropology were to endorse what for it would be a self-exploding psychologism, external norms must be granted priority when inquiry is concerned with how specific cultures shape human belief, self-representation and conduct. The forms assumed by subjectivity, in other words, are to be understood as a question of how the already instituted binds every psyche, thus rendering it a situated, culturally specific creature. Moreover, although the psyche provides some conditions of existence for the reproduction of any way of life, Levi-Strauss's insistence is valid. Hence a formula of sorts: that an individual psyche (or collection of psyches) is implicated in all racisms does not mean that a particular racist imaginary is explained when the fantasies, anxieties and defences sustaining it have been elucidated.

Now, psychoanalysis has long suspected that racism of whatever kind cannot be accounted for without reference to the 'early' splitting and projecting psyche. To which may be added, as Dalal (ibid.) among others have argued, that the existence of any racism requires idealization. For today's racism to be the product of an anxiety-laden, hate-filled opposition, the black other must not only be located as 'bad' (the effects of splitting and projection); requisite too is that the white 'in-group' is idealized and the black 'out-group' execrated so as to establish what, for any racist imaginary, is an inviolable boundary – one breached when cross-'racial' partnerships occur. Seen in this light, splitting, projection and idealization, capacities Kleinian theory locates as operating from the beginning of post-uterine life, are the means by which the loved in-group is originally differentiated from the hated out-group. Additionally, because our trio of psychical defences is responsible for the 'us-them' fantasmatic boundary, it is unsurprising that writing informed by Klein and Bion, as in Rustin (1991, 2001) for example, has tied the existence of racism to theses focusing on the 'primitive' – the Bionian adds, 'psychotic' – defences responsible for hate-filled, anxiety-provoking inter-group relations.

Here, we alight on a general psychoanalytical explanatory strategy in regard to racism, one by no means characteristic of Kleinian thought alone. The fantasizing infant/child (the boy of the Oedipus and castration for Freud, a dominance of paranoid-schizoid functioning for those informed by Kleinian thought) originates and maintains the boundary separating the white group and 'self' from feared and hated black others. And generally speaking, all racisms, including the kind from which black citizens in Western countries still suffer, are to be understood as productions of early fantasies which, when acted out, on occasion issue in racist violence and murder.

An important consideration for the psychoanalysis of racism now arises. When we are willing to grant that it is the 'unintegrated' infant/child in us which is responsible for the psychical possibility of a racist imaginary, does suspecting so entail the conclusion that racism must be an inevitable facet of the so-called human condition? Though many variants of psychoanalytical thought imply otherwise, there is reason to believe, on psychoanalytical grounds alone, that the answer must be 'no'. For if omnipotent projection, splitting and idealization are, as Kleinian thought argues, usually attenuated as the birth of a human subject ensues, there will be always be cases, in all likelihood many cases, for which racism has become impossible, and will remain so, because of identification with post-Oedipal authority figures (teachers, for example), disgust, reaction formation, and the awakening of adolescent ideals (see Kohut, 1977). Conversely, if the aforementioned trio of defences were to remain in their 'original' state, not only would the reality-testing powers of the ego be impossible, we would all be 'psychotic'. Expressed in Kleinian terms, then, that paranoid-schizoid functioning fuels any racist imaginary does not licence the conclusion 'racism is an inevitable feature of human sociality'. Racism, we may say, is inevitable only for those of us who, for whatever reasons, have not been able to bear the loss of the ideal breast and embrace the guilt required by the depressive struggle; for those among us who unconsciously deploy early-appearing defences so as to visit our internal discomfiture upon racialized others.

One implication of the foregoing is clear: it has been an error, a politically dangerous mistake too, to believe that all Western white men, because of particular histories of colonization that have only recently come to an end, *must* be racists (see Gordon, 1993, 2004). It contradicts the developmental animus of psychoanalytical thought simultaneously to hold that all racisms owe their existence to 'primitive' psychical processes yet that early operating defences are usually transformed as psycho-development ensues. That is to say, racism cannot be an inevitable feature of sociality, perhaps especially in a socio-political environment for which, regardless of skin colour, equality of treatment has become far more than an abstract principle of liberal democratic aspiration. And although it is plausible to assume that in-group/out-group relations of some kind or other will probably always exist, and for all that such relations have, in the historical societies known to us, sometimes been wedded to mutual suspicion, the racialization of human differences is another matter.

Returning to Levi-Strauss, what he does not say in his expected insistence on the anthropological priority of external norms to sentiment is that before any instituted norm can bind, a psyche *capable* of being bound by any ongoing, reproducible form of life must first be there. For psychoanalysis, it takes a psyche for most anything of the human kind to be possible – the reproduction of our species, any norm of conduct, the making of anything countable as art, the symbolic effects of any *rite de passage*, and any racism. Unless, therefore, we wish to rely on some version of behaviourism (even on social learning theory and its concept of observational learning) to advise how what is 'out there' gets 'in there', or on a Marxist or sociological conception of ideology with its emphasis on false consciousness rather than anxiety and desire, an account of the human material capable of being so bound is required. However, the over-arching problem hereabouts remains how psychoanalytically informed social thought is to valorize propositions stemming from incommensurable kinds of inquiry while also linking them.

On the one hand, all psyches are positioned subjects bound by external constraint for the (sociologico-) anthropological imagination. And because for Malinowski and Levi-Strauss psyches are creatures whose internal processes are circumscribed by the sentiments, beliefs and practices constructed by the forms of life in which they are embedded, racism can be understood as a culturally endorsed 'sentiment'. In addition, racism can also be rendered 'respectable' by state and media signifying practices. For psychoanalysis, on the other hand, all psyches exemplify the general psyche since the fashioning of human subjectivity instantiates universal processes of subject-formation. It is the very possibility, furthermore, of there being any binding sentiment and belief for a psyche that is of major concern to psychoanalysis, as evidenced in its therapeutic practice by the focus it accords (counter-) transference dynamics (see Foucault, ibid.).

An example will help to appreciate what is at stake. Imagine an English white man of 50 years of age, Michael, who is a blue collar worker, has had little formal education, and who voted for an extremely racist right-wing party at his country's local elections. Now suppose that an analysis focusing on class relations, the migration to the West of once-colonized peoples and the racist significations functioning in the wider culture produces a valuable account of why Michael is a racist. The analysis also considers the changing history of migration to Western countries over the last 50 years or so, patterns of (un)employment, racist state policies, media practices and the grotesque multi-conflation of 'asylum seeker' with 'refugee' and 'terrorist', which has occurred over the last few years. For all its explanatory power, however, what such an analysis cannot do, simply because such is not its domain, is advise how, for the sake of a 'full' account, we are to link Michael's working class position and racism with the history of his formation as a psychical subject. To put it differently, when concepts like socialization, observational learning and ideology are of little use hereabouts, the question 'why are Michael and other white men racists?' has not been answered, from the psychoanalytical perspective. Yet that judgement does not mean that psychoanalysis can advise of how class relations and other extra-psychical determinations are to be articulated with the maleficent desires fuelling today's white-black racism.

'External Reality', levels of analysis and the clinical situation

Thus far it has been argued that psychoanalysis and anthropology pass either by like proverbial ships in the night as modes of explanation. What for the one discourse is the primary methodological and episte-mological consideration is secondary for the other. And implicit in the foregoing is the conviction that psychoanalysis's focus on psychical processes cannot be seamlessly wedded to the social-historical dimensions of any racism since the universal purport of its claims makes such articulation impossible. Nevertheless, a 'disgraceful' failure is not to be attributed to psychoanalysis on this score, as doing so would rely on a naïve misunderstanding of its character. That, however, psychoanalysis is 'good' for some purposes and 'bad' for others leaves us with the task of addressing in what ways it is of use when the object of analysis is the racist imaginary of some white men. It will serve the aims of the chapter to comment now on how the 'external reality' to be accessed by the psyche is conceived by Freud.

'External reality' is understood by Freud as a question of how psychic energy, libido, must be 'bound' in and by the ego if the reality principle is to function. As Laplanche and Pontalis (1983) write, Freud uses 'binding'

> in a very general way and on comparatively distinct levels ... to denote an operation tending to restrict the free flow of excitations [that is, the unmediated pleasure sought by the id] to link ideas to one another [the function of the ego] and to constitute and maintain relatively stable forms.'
>
> (p. 50)

Freud (1911) counter-posed external reality to a psychical reality governed by the pleasure principle, and proposed that the psyche is characterized by two kinds of functioning: by a primary process taking no account of external reality and a secondary process at the behest of the ego – that 'relatively stable form'. Pertinent is that history, in the sense of recognizable 'times', as well as the subjectivities fashioned by different cultures, are thereby obliterated. In consequence, what the sociologist, historian and anthropologist respectively understand as different societies, periods, and ways of life is undercut by Freud's emphasis on the existence of the one and only 'external reality'. More than anything else, it has been this emphasis on a universally extant external reality, one the positivist in the suspicious Freud did not question, which has been responsible for the 'inability' of psychoanalysis to conceive that many historical racisms have existed.

Other emphases in Freud have exacerbated the problem. His conception of external reality is, as Gilman (1993) has argued, laden not only by racist assumptions. As reading Stocking (1987), the historian of anthropological discourse, suggests, Freud's notion of external reality is also tied to the Jacob's ladder of Western cultural achievement celebrated by the evolutionist anthropology of the nineteenth century. For example, several times in his writings, Freud 'theorises' that black men – what, on occasion, he calls 'the savage races' – are akin to the neurotics of his time, and to all children. Indeed, the subtitle to *Totem and Taboo*, published in 1913, reads 'Some points of agreement between the mental lives of savages and neurotics' (see Gordon, 2004, p. 295). Again, when writing of a 'herd instinct', one apparently expressed by 'a lack of emotional restraint, an incapacity for moderation and an inclination to exceed every limit in the expression of emotion', Freud is 'not surprised' to find evidence supporting his racism among 'savages' (Freud, 1921, p. 117). Reliant on historically specific imperialistic prejudices Freud learnt from reading the anthropology of his time, as well no doubt from local sources, these preposterous theses are superintended by a more general evolutionist claim running throughout his 'anthropological' writing: the developing 'civilization' of *Homo Sapiens* has required increasing repression of infantile pleasures; parenthetically, a gathering repressive power which Marcuse (1986), dissatisfied with Freud's ahistorical conceptions of the ego and the reality principle, reconceived as the 'desublimated repression' demanded by the 'advanced' capitalism of his time. The point is that Freud's portrait of humankind, tragic yet liberating though it be, is attended by the racist assumption that the replacement of superstition by science has required costly discontents the 'primitive peoples' do not share. Not only then is 'external reality' ever one and the same for the founder of psychoanalysis; it is dehistoricized in such a way that he appears consoled by the belief that the present, the society of his day, owes its existence to the increasing silence of the perverse-savage child in 'western' men of his class and time (for further discussion of the argument presented by Freud in *Totem and Taboo* and its usefulness for current social critique, See Gaitanidis's 'The Phantom of the Primal Father', Chapter 5 in this book).

What should we conclude? Whatever else, it would be an over-interpretation, as well as a 'projection' of human-scientific reason, to advise that Freud's manner of elaborating psychoanalytical thought was founded on racist claims. Just as it is a *non sequitur* to jump from 'some white men are racist' to 'all are racist', so it is to conclude that 'Freudian thought is racist' because 'the racism of his time informs his thought'. Nonetheless, that the racism is there is unacceptable for those of us who continue to endorse the project of liberal democracy; for the 'us' who will hold onto the hope of achieving a country in which skin colour will have become as irrelevant to our life chances as being born with blue eyes and blond hair.

Perspicuous too is that Freud collapsed levels of analysis – the levels of the psychically fashioned individual, the group-psychical, the politico-economic, and the historical. Remember our fictional Michael, in this regard: that his racism is his and, in a crucial sense, his alone, renders it a poisonous passion perhaps only intricate clinical attention will transform. I will return to this point. For the time being, note that because Michael's racism is a shared passion underpinned by group-psychical processes, he most likely receives conscious and unconscious reinforcement from similar men. In addition, that his racism is the rotten fruit of significations inseparable from the economic history of Western capitalism and the post-colonial politics of Western states must be borne in mind. After all, it is not only Michael and men like him who are responsible for the white-black racist imaginary of our time. In short, Michael's racism, whatever is to be concluded about how it has 'got into him', is not the product of psychical dynamics alone; it has sprung from a kaleidoscope of 'causes', for all that it speaks of his psychical formation.

We may wonder now if other than 'classical' Freudian theory can do better vis-à-vis distinguishing, and respecting, the levels of analysis involved in explaining contemporary white man's racism. For Tuckwell (in Wheeler, 2006), Kleinian thought is 'of fundamental importance in understanding race and culture and elucidating complex racial and cultural dynamics at both a personal level and a societal level' (p. 147). One appreciates why that is said. It was Klein (1946) who first elaborated the concept of projective identification as inaugurating an aggressive object relation, and Bion (1957, 1959) who revolutionized Klein's under-standing by means of his conception of the 'container' (in the first instance, the 'good' breast) and 'contained' (the infant's terror of frag-mentation). As can be seen from Rustin's analysis of the inter-psychical character of racialization (1991) and his comments on post-apartheid South Africa (2001, p. 121), Bion's reformulation has proven highly influential for the psychoanalysis of racism. With Bion in tow, we might say that Michael's racism has the following inter-psychical dynamic: he repudiates 'parts' of himself by means of a projection which the recipient introjects, the psychical effect of which is calamitous: black men are colonized by a persecutory anxiety not their own.

Again, what should we conclude? While Bion's intriguing and clini-cally influential reformulation of projective identification has served our understanding of the dynamics operating in any racist imaginary, it has not resolved the major problem identified here for the psycho-analysis of racism. How is the emphasis on (inter-) psychical dynamics cogently to be linked with the occurrence of *different* historical rac-isms? That remains a serious theoretical problem, on two counts. First, because psychoanalysis is obliged to conceive of all human subjects as fashioned by the same processes of psychical formation, it 'freezes' subjectivity as always one and the same. Freud (1923) exemplified that conceptual strategy by rendering the id impervious to the influence of the 'outside' – an insistence which, albeit marshalled to support the specificity of unconscious motivation, is incommensurable with the anthropological insistence that forms of life radically shape subjectivity. Or, with our focus on Kleinian thought, we could say that, because it posits idealization, projection and splitting as existing from the beginning of life, it undercuts the anthropological insistence on the effectivity of always particular instituted ways of rearing children.

Second, how is extrapolation from clinical practice with often highly distressed individuals to claims of general applicability to be justified? To the fore in posing that question, to which I shall briefly return in the final section of the chapter, is the hybrid character of psychoanalysis as simultaneously a modern therapeutic practice and a universally applicable theory of the psychical differentiation introduced by the processes serving human enculturation. As a practice based in the clinical situation, psychoanalysis is entitled to formulate propositions of the kind, 'therapeutic practice with Michael established that his racism was linked with anxieties about his masculinity and identification with a working class father regularly humiliated by periods of unemployment'. Predicated on *working* with him in a manner focusing on the (counter-)transference dynamics of Michael's case, that sort of claim is legitimate. Claims of the kind, 'today's white-black racism is born of generally operating psychical processes' are not – or, at least not so on the same basis. In the former case we have a proposition formulated on the basis of the affective struggles of a particular man, in the latter an extrapolation from clinical practice applied to racism as a general psychical and social-historical phenomenon.

It is of interest now that Cornelius Castoriadis spent 40 years or so attempting to reconfigure psychoanalytical theory in a way respectful of historical time, cultural affiliation and Marxist thought (Castoriadis, 1978, 1984). He did so by conceiving of two distinct orders of determination as governing human existence, namely, the psychical domain (the 'radical imaginary') and the social-historical domain (the 'social imaginary' – the realm of social-historical significations). Nevertheless the re-elaboration of 'classical' psychoanalytical thought undertaken by Castoriadis poses much the same problem as we have encountered in Freud and Klein. Since Castoriadis's thought is complex, informed by his philosophical erudition, and deeply critical of how Freud and other major contributors (including Klein) to the theory of psychoanalysis have sought to corral the radical imaginary by concepts inappropriate to what he argued is the 'creativity' and 'flux' of psychical life, let us simply note that Whitebook's critique is apt.

In his response to Castoriadis, Whitebook (1995) focuses on the 'out-there, in-there' problem so as to inquire if the human infant could at first be a self-enclosed psychism, as Castoriadis contends. The infant cannot be an internally undifferentiated monad cut-off from any possible external world, Whitebook argues, since if the converse were the case, it is inconceivable how any *infans*, black or white, could ever become a situated, social subject. How could anything of social-historical determination (the racist belief in the superiority of whites, for example) 'get in'? We may add that if all infants were to begin their congress with human association so, it is unthinkable why any of us, whatsoever our historical time and cultural home, would not be psychotic. Unthinkable too would be how Castoriadis, a white man versed in the ways of philosophy, psychoanalysis and revolutionary politics, could have written anything at all.

To be fair to Castoriadis, he has not been the first, nor will he be the last, to propose a novel thesis concerning how psychoanalysis is to conceive of what it is like to be an infant awaiting the 'catastrophe' of sociality. None the less, it is plain that his thought, like Freud's and Klein's, has not furnished what a 'full' account of today's racist imaginary requires – bridging concepts capable of connecting universally operating psychical processes (the domain of psychoanalytical theory) with the instituted practices (the anthropologico-sociological domain) bearing on every psyche. Remember Levi-Strauss: 'Social behaviour is not produced spontaneously by each individual, under the influence of the emotions of the present.'

Conclusion: Achieving a better country

'Race' has been a terrain of political engagement in many Western countries for many years now; rightly so, because white men's racism advises that we have some way to go before we can achieve a better country. Saying so is not to overlook the fact that, in response to the injuries perpetrated by racism, 'multiculturalism' continues to serve as a valuable means of respecting differences in communal belonging a pluralist liberal democracy need not fear. However, although educational practices informed by multiculturalist ethics have done some good, a recent development, one hard to date precisely, has appeared, in part as an unintended consequence of the rise of the modern anthropological imagination. Providing testimony to the recursive character of the human sciences, to how 'theory' can leak into how we experience ourselves, 'culture' has now assumed at least two meanings. There is the technical acceptation of the term, as defined by anthropological discourse, and its demotic, potentially explosive, sense. As young black men can say now (or so this teacher imagines them saying), 'culture is ours, the background I share with you, brother, something that identifies us as different from our white counterparts, and unites us in the face of the racism we experience, most every day of our lives'.

This development is of singular political significance. Although the (sub-)culture many black boys and young men share now probably functions as a collective resource for the contestation of their humiliation, it is also a danger for our new country. As collective resource, their culture has supported fashioning identities from what we may plausibly hypothesize on psychoanalytical grounds is, in many cases, a furiously proud reaction against the humiliation of their parents. That development needs to be respected, and understood. On the other hand, there is a danger because the country yet to be born could develop in two ways. As global capitalism gathers momentum, and as long as the mal-distribution of income, wealth and life chances remains unaddressed in meaningful ways, our new country could become a ghettoized monstrosity. There will be plenty for the wealthy and powerful, perhaps a modest plenty for a new heterogeneous majority, including black families, and growing alienation and resentment for an 'underclass'. Is that the kind of country we want? Although white men's racism will not have disappeared (by what means could that miracle be achieved?), the other possibility is that it will have been checked, at least that, by a state territory refusing to base any policy, whatsoever the political gains of doing otherwise might be, on complicity with the anxieties of the racist imaginary of our time.

What of psychoanalysis, in this respect? 'Culture' as contestation and danger is in part a welcome development, for it suggests what needs to be done in terms of the reconfiguration of psychoanalytical thought. For the psychoanalysis of the future, it will not be that 'external reality' will have gone – certainly not the realities we now struggle with, everyday. Rather, because the all-embracing character of the claims psychoanalytical thought has proposed vis-à-vis external reality will have been exploded by black young men's suffering, it will have become *de rigueur* not to assume that all male creatures have the same psychical obstacles to overcome in fashioning a tolerably fulfilling life in late-modern societies. Correlatively, because it will have become unremarkable to ask, 'of whose external reality are you writing?' and 'who, if anybody, is entitled to speak for all in our ethnically diverse country?', turning psychoanalytical suspicion back on itself will be virtuous. We will have grown used to asking: 'What (counter-) transference is at stake in that conception of external reality? What is being idealized? What marginalization is being denied there? What values are reinforced by envisioning the good life in that way?' (See O'Carroll, 2007).

Finally, who knows now, but it may prove useful, if only indirectly and to some minor degree, to extend the postmodern suspicion that the politics of theory is as significant as the 'truth' our best thinking attempts to capture, to psychoanalysis itself. Does psychoanalytical thought imagine a unitary culture – an 'out there' presupposing that white men's racism is explained by focusing on psychical processes alone? Part of this suspicious strategy, moreover, will involve the revitalization of psychoanalysis in a particular way. Because the claims it renders of its therapeutic practice are one matter, the 'application' of such claims to the social-historical domain, another, it remains unclear what role, if any, psychoanalytical inquiry can play in informing political action directed to the achievement of our better country. As already indicated, a claim of the kind 'all racisms are in part the products of individually and collectively deployed defences' is not the same kind of claim the psychoanalyst – by extension, the psychoanalytical psychotherapist and psychodynamic counsellor – can make of working clinically with such a man as Michael.

That is not to say that the latter kind of claim is useless, for all that it can be speculative. What it is to advise is that, because psychoanalysis has a particular discursive character, we will serve it well by continuing to raise the question of its utility for helping us to achieve a better, less racist, country.

Conclusion

Anastasios Gaitanidis

In this book we employed different theoretical avenues and perspectives with which to think critically, clinically and theoretically about masculinity. We also approached masculinity from a point of view that understands gender as fluid and multiple. In doing so, we attempted to reposition masculinity firmly within the larger field of gendered subjectivities, recognising all the essential contradictions, complexities, and multiplicities of the masculine position.

For this reason, we proposed alternative ways of conceptualising the position of the male which do not always involve phallic potency and/or paternal prohibition. We suggested, therefore, that maleness can emerge from a more subtle exchange than the one-way phallic penetration of some ambient empty vaginal space waiting to be procreative. There are a whole range of intra/other pressures that generate the male-effect – in particular those involving the wrestling couple – whose 'contusive' process produces a varied and complex mix of pleasure and pain.

We also challenged the homosexual-heterosexual divide by pointing out that since perversion is at the centre of the psychoanalytic account of sexuality, all forms of male sexual desire and practice spring from the same psychical root. Additionally, we explored the importance of men's friendships with other men and suggested contemporary psychoanalytic theories which offer the possibility for men to 'play' with desire and identification. Yet, we also noted how psychoanalysis is still haunted by the legacy of the phallus, the privileging of the breast and/or the mother-child dyad which disregard or repudiate the relational dynamics of maleness and fatherhood.

Moreover, we argued that, on a cultural and psychoanalytic level, fathers seem to gain publicity because they sexually abuse children, subject them to physical violence, and avoid their financial and emotional responsibilities. There is comparatively little cultural and psychoanalytic emphasis on a loving father who is actively involved in the child-rearing process. In other words, there is a significant absence of a benevolent male role model who can actively contribute to children's care.

In addition, the social 'function of the father' that served to frame and organise men's desires and ambitions seems to become increasingly weak and unstable. In the absence of any viable alternatives, men identify with grandiose, omnipotent paternal figures so as to satisfy their need for simultaneous assumption of and submission to authority.

This is closely connected to Freud's insight into the traumatic bases of authority, his focus on the fear, need for protection, and love that runs through the relation to the father. Subsequent psychoanalytic theorists became increasingly aware of the role of the mother, eventually realising her centrality. Yet it is important that we do not drop Freud's view of the father as the protector of early childhood. Only this makes certain male patients' internal conflicts and ambivalence comprehensible. They not only fear their father, they also love him, and their love deepens and complicates their fear. Freud drove this point home with his speculative myth of the murder of the primal father. But what makes this story worth listening to are the cases of men whose lives have been profoundly affected by the absence of a 'strong' concrete paternal figure who could help them reconcile their fear with their love so as not to have to resort to enthusiastic identifications with tyrannical, God-like authority figures (i.e., primal fathers).

Furthermore, we critically examined how the current socio-political climate has seriously undermined the emotional life of men whose best hope for connection with other human beings lies in detachment. This is because the current social positioning of the male is marked by the bargaining for profit and power where tender emotions have no place. It is precisely this requirement to survive without emotional attachments that is the crucial element of the conventional 'rites of passage' which justify the use of shame and humiliation as a means of strengthening and consolidating male identity.

These humiliating experiences are intensely experienced by men who would commit horrifying acts of violence rather than being exposed to shame and loss of self-respect. However, despite the violent nature of the external threat of shame and humiliation, it is also the threat from *within* masculine identity, created by its own internal instabilities, that is potentially problematic. Due to the uncertainty that these instabilities produce, men feel increasingly uncomfortable with their sense of maleness and seek to distance themselves from it. Thus, instead of comprehending and effectively dealing with the aspects of their masculinity that they perceive as bothersome (e.g., homosexual erotic desires or feelings of inferiority), they want to eradicate these 'negative' aspects altogether. As a result, they either over-repress or aggressively evacuate these 'harmful' elements – that is to say, they end up producing considerable damage to themselves and others through their homophobic and/or racist attitudes.

Nevertheless, we also noted how certain men keep from destroying their own lives and the lives of other people, how they absent themselves from the tradition of male violence, how they decline the seduction of racist revenge. The implication here is that some men are able to recognise themselves as the subjects of violence and employ their capacity for critical reasoning so as not to perpetuate this violence.

However, men's capacity for critical reasoning is not enough without the simultaneous broadening of their sphere of experience and perception to include emotion and acknowledgement of desire. For this reason, the contribution of psychoanalysis to the understanding of male identity remains invaluable. This is because psychoanalysis is born out of reflection upon men's (and women's) experiences of suffering, defeat, loss and mourning. What is unique in it is a language which is centred on recognising the importance not only of men's need for authority and control but also their need for love and dependency and their experiences of fear and vulnerability. These needs and experiences are not alternatives to authority and control but rather their dark, excluded complement. And it is only by identifying and engaging with this 'dark, excluded complement' that men will be able to endure the disintegration of their traditional selves and find the strength to reformulate their identities.

References

Adorno, T. W. (1951). 'Freudian Theory and the Pattern of Fascist Propaganda'. In A. Arato and E. Gebhardt (eds), *The Essential Frankfurt School Reader*. Oxford: Blackwell, 1978.

Adorno, T. W., Frenkel-Brunswick, F., Levinson, D., and Sanford, R. (1950). *The Authoritarian Personality*. New York: Harper and Row.

Anzieu, D. (1986). *Freud's Self Analysis*. New York: International Universities Press.

Aristotle (1962). *The Nicomachean Ethics*. Ed. H. Tredennick, Trans. J. A. K. Thomson, with an Introduction by Jonathan Barnes. London: Penguin Classics.

Benjamin, J. (1988). *The Bonds of Love*. London: Virago.

Benjamin, J. (1995). *Like Subjects, Love Objects*. New Haven, CT: Yale University Press.

Bion, W. (1957). 'Differentiation of the Psychotic from the Non-Psychotic Personalities'. *The International Journal of Psycho-Analysis*, 38, pp. 266–75.

Bion, W. (1959). 'Attacks on Linking'. *International Journal of Psycho-Analysis*, 40, pp. 308–15.

Boothby, R. (2005). *Sex on the Couch – What Freud Still Has to Teach us About Sex and Gender*. New York, London: Routledge.

Boswell, J. (1980). *Christianity, Social Intolerance, and Homosexuality*. Chicago and London: University of Chicago Press.

Butler, J. (1993). *Bodies that Matter: On the Discursive Limits of Sex*. New York and London: Routledge.

Butler, J. (2004). *Undoing Gender*. New York and London: Routledge.

Castiglione, B. (1528). *Il Libro del Cortigiano*. Edited by B. Maier Turin, 1964.

Castoriadis, C. (1984). *Crossroads in the Labyrinth*. Brighton, England: The Harvester Press.

Castoriadis, C. (1987). *The Imaginary Institution of Society*. Oxford: Polity Press.

Castoriadis, C. (1997). *World in Fragments – Writings on Politics, Society, Psychoanalysis*. Ed. and Trans. D. A. Curtis. Stanford, CA: Stanford University Press.

Chodorow, N. (1978). *The Reproduction of Mothering*. Berkeley: University of California Press.

Chodorow, N. (1994). *Femininities, Masculinities, Sexualities: Freud and Beyond*. New York and London: Free Association Books.

Clewell, T. (2004). 'Mourning Beyond Melancholia: Freud's Psychoanalysis of Loss', *Journal of the American Psychoanalytic Association*. Vol. 52, no. 1, pp. 43–67.

Cohen, J. (2005). *How to Read Freud*. London: Granta Books.

Cohen, J. (2007). 'I-not-I: Narcissism Beyond the One and the Other'. In A. Gaitanidis (ed.), *Narcissism – A Critical Reader*. London: Karnac.

Copjec, J. (1996). 'Introduction: Evil in the Time of the Finite World'. In J. Copjec (ed.), *Radical Evil*. London: Verso.

Dalal, F. (2002). *Race, Colour and the Processes of Racialization – New Perspectives from Group Analysis, Psychoanalysis and Sociology*. London and New York: Routledge.

Davis, M. and Wallbridge, D. (1981). *Boundary and Space: An Introduction to the Work of D. W. Winnicott*. London: Karnac.

Deleuze, G. and Guattari, F. (1972). *L'Anti-Oedipe*. Paris: Minuit.

Derrida, J. (1985). 'Prèjugès, devant la loi'. In J. Derrida, V. Descombes, G. Kortian, P. Lacoue-Labarthe, J.-F. Lyotard, J.-L. Nancy (eds), *La Facultè de Juger*. Paris: Minuit, pp. 87–140.

Dinnerstein, D. (1976). *The Mermaid and the Minotaur*. New York: Harper and Row.

Domenici, T. and Lesser, R. (eds) (1995), *Disorientating Sexuality*. London: Routledge.

Eagleton, T. (1985). *Literary Theory: An Introduction*. Oxford: Blackwell.

Evans, D. (1996). *Dictionary of Lacanian Psychoanalysis*. London: Routledge.

Flax, J. (1991). *Thinking Fragments: Psychoanalysis, Feminism and Post-modernism in the Contemporary West*. Berkeley, CA: University of California Press.

Fletcher, J. (1999). 'Introduction: Psychoanalysis and the Question of the Other' – Editor's Introduction to J. Laplanche (1999a). *Essays on Otherness*, London and New York: Routledge.

Foucault, M. (1970). *The Order of Things*. London: Tavistock.

Foucault, M. (1981). *The History of Sexuality, Vol. 1: The Will to Knowledge*. London: Pelican Books.

Foucault, M. (1986). *The History of Sexuality, Vol. 2: The Use of Pleasure*. London: Viking.

Foucault, M. (1990). *The History of Sexuality, Volume 3: The Care of the Self*, London: Penguin Books.

Freud, S. (1905). 'Three Essays on the Theory of Infantile Sexuality'. *The Standard Edition of the Complete Psychological Works of Sigmund Freud*, Vol. VII. Trans. and Ed. J. Strachey. London: Hogarth Press (hereafter *SE*).

Freud, S. (1905). 'Jokes and their Relation to the Unconscious'. *SE* VIII.

Freud, S. (1910). 'Leonardo da Vinci and a Memory of his Childhood'. *SE* IX.

Freud, S. (1911). 'Formulations on the Two Principles of Mental Functioning'. *SE* XXII.

Freud, S. (1911). 'Psycho-Analytic Notes on an Autobiographical Account of a Case of Paranoia (Dementia Paranoides)'. *SE* XII.

Freud, S. (1912–13). 'Totem and Taboo'. *SE* VII.

Freud, S. (1914). 'On Narcissism – An Introduction'. *SE* XIV.

Freud, S. (1915). 'Instincts and Their Vicissitudes'. *SE* XIV.

Freud, S. (1915). 'The Metapsychological Papers'. *SE* XIV.

Freud, S. (1916). 'On Transience'. *SE* XIV.

Freud, S. (1916–17). 'Introductory Lectures on Psycho-Analysis'. *SE* XVI.

Freud, S. (1917). 'Mourning and Melancholia'. *SE* XIV.

Freud, S. (1921). 'Group Psychology and the Analysis of the Ego'. *SE* XVIII.

Freud, S. (1923). 'The Ego and the Id'. *SE* XIX.

Freud, S. (1926). 'The Question of Lay Analysis'. *SE* XX.

Freud, S. (1927). 'The Future of an Illusion'. *SE* XXI.

Freud, S. (1930). 'Civilization and its Discontents'. *SE* XXI.

Freud, S. (1933). 'New Introductory Lectures on Psychoanalysis'. *SE* XXII.

Frosh, S. (1994). *Sexual Difference: Masculinity and Psychoanalysis*. London and New York: Routledge.

Frosh, S. (2002). *After Words: The Personal in Gender, Culture and Psychotherapy*. London: Palgrave Macmillan.

Gaitanidis, A. (ed.) with Curk, P. (2007). *Narcissism: A Critical Reader*. London: Karnac.

Gellner, E. (1981). *The Psychoanalytic Movement*. London: Pantheon.

Giddens, A. (1991). *Modernity and Self-Identity: Self and Society in the late Modern Age*. Oxford: Polity Press.

Gilligan, J. (2000). *Violence: Reflections on Our Deadliest Epidemic*. London: Jessica Kingsley Publishers.

Gilman, S. (1993). *Freud, Race, and Gender*. New Jersey: Princeton University Press.

Godard, J. L. (1998). *Histoire(s) du Cinema*. Paris: Gallimard.

Gordon, D. (1981). *The National Gallery, London: 100 Great Paintings*. Kettering: The George Press.

Gordon, P. (1993). 'Souls in Armour: Thoughts on Psychoanalysis and Racism'. *The British Journal of Psychotherapy*, 20th Anniversary Edition 1984–2004, 21, no. 2, 2004, pp. 277–94.

Gordon, P. (2004). 'Psychoanalysis and Racism: Some Further Thought's'. *The British Journal of Psychotherapy*, 21, no. 2, 2004, pp. 294–98.

Green, A. (2001). *Life Narcissism, Death Narcissism*. Trans. A. Weller. London: Free Association Books.

Greenberg, J. and Mitchell, S. (1983). *Object Relations in Psychoanalytic Theory*, Boston, MA: Harvard University Press.

Greenson, R. (1968). 'Disidentifying from Mother: Its Special Importance for the Boy'. In *Explorations in Psychoanalysis*. New York: International Universities Press, pp. 305–12.

Heaney, S. (trans.) (2008). *Beowulf*. New York: Norton.

Hinshelwood, R. (1989). *A Dictionary of Kleinian Thought*. London and New York: Free Association Books.

Hirst, P. Q. (1979) *On Law and Ideology*, London: Macmillan.

Hirst, P. Q. and Woolley, P. (1982). *Social Relations and Human Attributes*. London: Tavistock.

Institute of Social Research (1973). 'The Family'. In *Aspects of Sociology*. Trans. J. Viertel. London: Heinemann

Jacoby, M. (1984). *The Analytic Encounter: Transference and Human Relationship*. New York: Inner Space.

Jones, E. (1964). 'Mother Right and the Sexual Ignorance of Savages'. E. Jones, *Essays in Applied Psychoanalysis 2*. New York: International Universities Press. Republished as *Psycho-Myth, Psycho-History* (1974). New York: Hillstone.

Jones, E. (1980). *Sigmund Freud: Life and Work*. London: The Hogarth Press.

Jung, C. (1954). *Psychological Aspects of the Mother Archertype*. Collected Works, Vol 9(i). Translated by R. F. C. Hull. London: Routledge and Kegan Paul, 1968.

Jung, C. (1955–6). *Mysterium Conjunctionis: An Enquiry into the Separation and Synthesis of Psychic Opposites in Alchemy*. Collected Works, Vol. 14. Translated by R. F. C. Hull. London: Routledge & Kegan Paul, 1968.

Jung, C. (1959). *Aion: Researches in the Phenomenology of Self*. Collected Works, Vol. 9(ii). Translated by R.F.C. Hull. London: Routledge & Kegan Paul, 1968.

Jung, C. G. (1912 [1951]). *Psychology of the Unconscious*. London: Routledge.

Klein, M. (1923). 'The Role of the School in the Libidinal Development of the Child'. In *The Writings of Melanie Klein, Vol. 1*. London: Hogarth Press.

Klein, M. (1926). 'The Psychological Principles of Early Analysis'. In *The Writings of Melanie Klein, Vol. 1*. London: The Hogarth Press.

Klein, M. (1927). 'Criminal Tendencies in Normal Children'. In *The Writings of Melanie Klein, Vol. 1*. London: The Hogarth Press.

Klein, M. (1933). 'The Early Development of Conscience in the Child'. In Sandor Lorand, (ed.), *Psycho-Analysis Today*. New York: Covici-Friede.

Klein, M. (1937). *Love, Guilt and Reparation*. In *The Writings of Melanie Klein, Vol. 1*. London: The Hogarth Press.

Klein, M. (1946). 'Notes on Some Schizoid Mechanisms'. *The International Journal of Psycho-Analysis*, 27, pp. 99–110. Republished (1952) in M. Klein, P. Heimann, S. Isaacs and J. Riviere (eds), *Developments in Psycho-Analysis*. The Hogarth Press, pp. 292–320.

Klein, M. (1946–63). *Envy and Gratitude and Other Works 1946–63*. New York: Delta New York, 1977.

Kohut, H. (1972). *The Search for the Self*. New York: International University Press.

Kohut, H. (1977). *The Restoration of the Self*. New York: International Universities Press.

Kristeva, J. (1980). *Desire in Language: a Semiotic Approach to Literature and Art*. Oxford: Blackwell.

Kristeva, J. (1983). 'Freud and Love'. In T. Moi (ed.), *The Kristeva Reader*. Oxford: Balckwell.

Kuhn, T. (1962). *The Structure of Scientific Revolutions*. Chicago: The University of Chicago Press.

Lacan, J. (1937). 'The Mirror-Stage as Formative of the "I" as Revised in Psycho-analytic Experience'. Trans. Alan Sheridan, in *Ecrits*, London: Tavistock, 1977.

Lacan, J. (1977). *Ecrits – A Selection*. London: Routledge.

Lacan, J. (1992). *The Seminar of Jacques Lacan, Book VII, The Ethics of Psychoanalysis*. Ed. Jacques-Alain Miller, Trans. Dennis Porter. New York: W.W. Norton.

Lagache, D. (1993). *The Work of Daniel Lagache*. London: Karnac.

Laplanche, J. (1976). *Life and Death in Psychoanalysis*. Trans. and Intro. J. Mehlman. Baltimore: Johns Hopkins University Press.

Laplanche, J. (1987). *New Foundations for Psychoanalysis*. Trans. David Macey. Oxford: Basil Blackwell, 1989.

Laplanche, J. (1993). *Le Fourvoiement Biologisant de la Sexualite chez Freud*. Paris: Empecheurs de Penser en Rond.

Laplanche, J. (1999a). *Essays on Otherness*, Ed. John Fletcher, London and New York: Routledge.

Laplanche, J. (1999b). 'A Short Treatise on the Unconscious', in Laplanche 1999a, pp. 52–83.

Laplanche, J. (1999c). 'Implantation, Intromission', in Laplanche, 1999a, pp. 133–7.

Laplanche, J. (1999d). 'Seduction, Persecution, Revelation', in Laplanche, 1999a, pp. 166–96.

Laplanche, J. (1999e). *The Unconscious and the Id: A volume of Laplanche's Probematiques*. London: Rebus Press.

Laplanche, J. and Pontalis, J.-B. (1983). *The Language of Psycho-Analysis*. London: The Hogarth Press and the Institute of Psycho-Analysis.

Laplanche, J. and Pontalis, J.-B. (1986). 'Fantasy and the Origins of Sexuality'. In V. Burgin (ed.), *Formations of Fantasy*. London.

Lasch, C. (1979). *The Culture of Narcissism: American Life in an Age of Diminishing Expectations*. New York: W. W. Norton & Co.

Lewes, K. (1989). *The Psychoanalytic Theory of Male Homosexuality*. New York: Basic Books.

Maguire, M. (2005). 'The Website 'Girl': Contemporary Theories about Male 'Femininity' '. *British Journal of Psychotherapy*, Vol. 22, No. 1.

Malinowski, B. (1937). *Sex and Repression in Savage Society*. London: Routledge and Kegan Paul.

Marcuse, H. (1986). *One-Dimensional Man – Studies in the Ideology of Advanced Industrial Society*. London: Ark Paperbacks.

Mitchell, J. (2000). *Mad Men and Medusas – Reclaiming Hysteria and the Effects of Sibling Relations on the Human Condition*. London: The Penguin Press.

Miyasaki, D. (2003). 'The Evasion of Gender in Freudian Fetishism'. *Psychoanalysis, Culture, and Society*, Vol. 8, No. 2, pp. 289–98.

Nehemas, A. (1985). *Life as Literature*, Boston, MA: Harvard University Press.

O'Carroll. L. (2007). 'Narcissism, Primal Seduction, and the Psychoanalytic Search for a Good Life'. In A. Gaitanidis with P. Curk (eds) *Narcissism – A Critical Reader*. London: Karnac.

O'Connor, N. and Ryan, J. (1993). *Wild Desires & Mistaken Identities (Lesbianism and Psychoanalysis)*. London: Virago Press.

Philips, A. (1999). *Darwin's Worms*. London: Faber and Faber.

Phillips, A. (2000a). 'Narcissism – For and Against'. In *Promises Promises*. London: Faber & Faber.

Phillips, A. (2000b). 'On Translating a Person'. In *Promises Promises*. London: Faber & Faber.

Plummer, K. (ed.) (1981). *The Making of the Modern Homosexual*. London: Routledge and Kegan Paul.

Richards, V. with Wilce, G. (eds) (1997). *Fathers, Families and the Outside World*. London: Karnac.

Rorty, R. (1989). *Contingency, Irony, and Solidarity*. Cambridge: Cambridge University Press.

Rose, N. (1998). *Inventing our Selves: Psychology, Power and Personhood*. Cambridge: Cambridge University Press.

Rustin, M. (1991). *The Good Society and the Inner World: Psychoanalysis, Politics and Culture*. London: Verso.

Rustin, M. (2001). *Reason and Unreason – Psychoanalysis, Science and Politics*. London: Continuum.

Rycroft, C. (1975). *A Critical Dictionary of Psychoanalysis* (2nd edition). London: Penguin Books.

Sandler, J. (ed.) (1988). *Projection, Identification, Projective Identification*. London: Karnac.

Segal, H. (1950). 'Some Aspects of the Analysis of a Schizophrenic', *International Journal of Psycho-Analysis* 31, pp. 268–78; republished (1981) in *The Work of Hanna Segal*. New York: Jason Aronson.

Segal, H. (1957). 'Notes on Symbol Formation', *International Journal of Psycho-Analysis* 38, pp. 391–7; republished (1981) in *The Work of Hanna Segal* (ibid.).

Sellars, W. (1967). *Science, Perception and Reality*. London: Routledge and Kegan Paul.

Soulliere, D. (2006). 'Wrestling with Masculinity', *Sex Roles*, July 2006.

Spence, D. (1994). *The Rhetorical Voice of Psychoanalysis: Displacement of Evidence by Theory*. Boston, MA: Harvard University Press.

Stanton, M. (1993). 'Psychic Contusion'. *British Journal of Psychotherapy*, Summer 1993.

Stanton, M. (1996). 'Imagos and the Problem of the Imaginary'. In M. Stanton and D. Reason (eds), *Teaching Transference*. London: Rebus.

Stanton, M. (1997). *Out of Order: Clinical Work and Unconscious Process*. London: Rebus.

Stern, D. (1985). *The Interpersonal Word of the Infant: A View from Psychoanalysis and Developmental Psychology*. London: Karnac.

Stocking, G. W. (1987). *Victorian Anthropology*. New York: The Free Press. London: Collier Macmillan.

Stoller, R. (1975). *Perversion – The Erotic Form of Hatred*. London: Karnac.

Stubrin, J. P. (1994). *Sexualities and Homosexualities*. London: Karnac.

Tuckwell, G. (2006). 'Psychodynamic Counselling, "Race" and "Culture"'. In S. Wheeler (ed.), *Difference and Diversity in Counselling – Contemporary Psychodynamic Perspectives*. Basingstoke, UK and New York: Palgrave Macmillan

Whitebook, J. (1995). *Perversion and Utopia: A Study in Psychoanalysis and Critical Theory*. Cambridge, MA: The MIT Press.

Winnicott, D. W. (1990). *The Maturational Processes and the Facilitating Environment: Studies in the Theory of Emotional Development*. London: Karnac.

Zemeckis, R. (1997). *Beowulf*, DVD, Warner Brothers.

Index